GOD vs RELIGION

CREATION HOUSE
A STRANG COMPANY

EXPERIENCE A GREAT AWAKENING
PAUL DAVIS

God vs. Religion by Paul Davis
Published by Creation House
A Strang Company
600 Rinehart Road
Lake Mary, Florida 32746
www.creationhouse.com

This book or parts thereof may not be reproduced in any form, stored in a retrieval system, or transmitted in any form by any means—electronic, mechanical, photocopy, recording, or otherwise—without prior written permission of the publisher, except as provided by United States of America copyright law.

Publisher's note: The views expressed in this book are not necessarily the views held by the publisher.

Unless otherwise noted, Scripture quotations are from the New King James Version of the Bible. Copyright © 1979, 1980, 1982 by Thomas Nelson, Inc., publishers. Used by permission.

Scripture quotations marked KJV are from the King James Version of the Bible.

Cover design by Mark Labbe

Copyright © 2007 by Paul Davis
All rights reserved

Library of Congress Control Number: 2006936883
International Standard Book Number: 978-1-59979-085-8

First Edition

07 08 09 10 11 — 9 8 7 6 5 4 3 2 1

Printed in the United States of America

Acknowledgments

Thanks to my wife Karla for her unconditional love, support, and ongoing faithfulness. You have inwardly strengthened me personally whereby I can have a strong foundation from which to impact the nations. Thanks also for bringing a new world order to our house, creating a home where heaven can come to earth.

Thanks to Pastor Carlos Sarmiento and Pastor Amar Rambisoon for their magnificent ministries, fatherly love, prophetic insight, and impact upon my life. You have truly motivated me to excel in God to the fullness of my potential. Thanks for believing in me and empowering me to obey God without hesitation.

Thanks to my wonderful Dad and Mom (Paul and Paulette Davis) who were destined to have a son with the mantel and ministry like that of the apostle Paul. Your transparency, sincerity, humility, and sense of humor has repeatedly uplifted me. Thanks for loving, listening, and laughing with me.

Thanks to all the wonderful supporters of Dream-Maker Ministries, without which I could never fulfill my heavenly calling. Your prayers and generosity make it all happen. Know assuredly great is your reward in heaven.

Contents

	Introduction viii
1	Misrepresentation of the Master 1
2	Fig Leaves of Self-Sufficiency 8
3	Satan's Counterfeits and Deceptions............................... 13
4	Ignorance Is Not Bliss 27
5	Mouth Traps 31
6	Presents Versus Presence 46
7	Spirit and Truth.......................... 56
8	Religious Affiliation, Self-Exaltation, and Condemnation 63
9	Rigid and Frigid Rules 70
10	Dumb Doctrines and Convictions 81
11	Religion Is Static— God Is Spontaneous! 107
12	Relationship Over Religion 117
	Notes 123

Religiosity has its origins in the tree of knowledge and therein also are its limitations.

Religion says, "Do." Jesus says, "Done!"

Religion defends the dead before it celebrates the living.

The voice of religion says, "Shhh!" The voice of God says, "Lift up your voice!"

God goes up with a shout. Religion brings you down with a pout.

Religion labors to achieve a place of victory. Jesus already has the victory and bestows it upon us to enjoy freely.

Most Christians in North America and Europe are more intellectual than they are spiritual.

Most Christians live boring lives and rarely enter the realm of the Spirit to live adventurously by faith.

Until you live by faith, you have not truly begun to live.

As long as you remain in your religious boat with everyone else, you will never experience the miraculous.

To walk with Jesus, sometimes you have to leave your friends behind.

You were born an original. Don't die a copy.

Religion is cold as ice and never nice.

Religiosity is full of formality because it is void of spirituality.

Religion is slow and lethargic. The Holy Spirit is quick and powerful.

Religion is continually critical. The Holy Spirit is patient and helpful, understanding our weaknesses.

Religiosity is man-centered. Spirituality is God-centered.

Religion is focused on covering and preserving self. Spirituality, however, is enraptured with the Creator, enjoying His presence, partaking of His power, and co-laboring for His cause.

Introduction

I BEGAN WRITING THIS book as an answer to the questions of many people I have met who were unable to differentiate between religion and God. I heard one man ask a group of Christians, "Who created religion—God or man?" The fury and frenzy this enlightening question caused was fun to behold. Instead of speaking up to give the answer, I preferred to listen to the comments and enjoy the responses. In doing so I was better able to grasp where most of the people were spiritually.

Jesus asked questions to assess the understanding and discover the spiritual level of people. Knowing that many had differing opinions about Him, Jesus boldly asked: "Who do men say that I…am?" (Matt. 16:13). Upon getting feedback from a few honest and forthright folks, Jesus proceeded to ask a more probing and revealing question: "Who do you say that I am?" (Matt. 16:15).

Unlike most religious leaders and figureheads, Jesus was not the least bit intimidated or upset by honest answers. In fact, He preferred them. That is how Jesus answered people even if it meant offending them. Jesus did not hesitate to call Peter (one of His prized disciples) "Satan," when Peter sought to prevent Him from fulfilling His goal of dying for the sins of the world. Peter was mindful of earthly things and most likely wanted Jesus to liberate the Jews from Roman rule (Matthew 16:23; Acts 1:6).

Tree of Knowledge or Tree of Life?

We must ask ourselves: *If faced with the choice of knowledge or life, which one would I choose?* There were two trees in the Garden of Eden: the tree of knowledge and the tree of life (Gen. 2:9). Adam chose the wrong tree, and that is why our lives are limited in years and not eternal.

Why are we prone to seek knowledge over experiencing life? Could it be our personal pride and tendency toward self-sufficiency, which causes us to run after that which fills the head but leaves the heart empty? Religiosity has its origins in the tree of knowledge. God is not a Subject to be studied; He is a Person to know and experience.

I do not consider myself to be religious. The word *religious* conjures up an image of a bald monk dressed in black, with a cross around his neck and no smile on his face, who legalistically adheres to traditions and rules. I have never seen a religious person pictured smiling. It seems that most religious leaders prefer to look serious or in deep meditation.

I will never forget the Russian Orthodox priest in Moscow who hissed at us while we toured a cathedral observing the beautiful spiritual paintings within. I was with a group of young adults from America on a mission trip in 1992. The moment we began to excitedly express ourselves and happily remark about the various pieces of Christian art, the priest shushed us and told us to be quiet. We could not understand why. Shortly after the priest's first rebuke, we celebrated again. A harsh "Shhh!" suddenly reverberated across the cathedral from the priest.

I walked over to him and asked, "Why do we have to be quiet?" His reply shocked me. He said, "Because there are people buried beneath the church."

Isn't that interesting? The priest was more concerned about dead people than the living. And to me, that precisely defines the matter of religion. Religion defends the dead before it celebrates the living. Religion can never celebrate the living because it is dead. The liveliness of the living is an indictment against religion and further attests to its death. Religion would rather hush the happy than disturb the dead. Believers who succumb to this kind of religiosity will soon find themselves in bondage to religious legalism.

The voice of religion says, "Shhh!" The voice of God says, "Lift up your voice," "Speak on," "Be bold and very courageous," "Let the dead bury and care for the dead. You go and preach the gospel" (Acts 4:19–20, 24, 29–31; Josh. 1:6; Matt. 8:22, author's paraphrase).

"God has gone up with a shout" (Psalm 47:5); religion brings you down with a pout. When Jesus returns to the earth, He "will descend from heaven with a shout, with the voice of an archangel, and with the trumpet of God" (1 Thess. 4:16). When religion returns, it comes with a scowl of legalism and accusation.

I recall one priest who presided over the Anglican

Introduction

Church that my family attended when I was younger. He was such a perfectionist that when the Christmas service was taking place, he gave several people involved in the ceremony piercing looks as if to say, "Don't mess up!" Because the priest was so uptight, the people around him could not relax.

Religion always wants you to do more. Nothing is ever enough. The battle cry of religion is "Do, do, do!" Thankfully, Jesus already did it all when He died on the cross and said, "It is finished!" (John 19:30).

Religion labors to achieve a place of victory. Jesus, however, already has the victory and bestows it on us to enjoy freely. Religion wants you to work until you bleed. Jesus wants you to look unto Him and believe.

Cerebral or Spiritual?

I consider myself to be spiritual, just as the Creator is also Spirit, and not flesh and blood (John 4:24). Christians in North America and Europe tend to be more intellectual than spiritual. Many live by dollars and cents, listen to public opinion, seek to please people before God, and remain in their comfortable Christian country club. Yet God is not a brain, nor a philosophical Individual.

Top-heavy Christians live boring lives and rarely enter the realm of the Spirit to live adventurously by faith. Until you live by faith, you have not truly begun to live.

> The just shall live by faith.
> —Romans 1:17

God vs. Religion

Peter realized there was more to his spirituality than sitting in a religious boat with his friends. As long as you remain in your religious boat with everyone else, you will never experience the miraculous. Sometimes to walk with Jesus, you have to leave your friends behind. Peter did just that when he got out of the boat and walked on water with Jesus (Matt. 14:29).

When you remain true to the authentic person God made you to be, you will transcend all human barriers and build bridges cross-culturally. Groucho Marx once said, "You were born an original. Don't die a copy."[1] Religion is full of counterfeits, because it has no originality and is without divine inspiration. Religiosity is full of formality, because it is void of spirituality. Religiosity cleaves to liturgy, because it does not know the Holy Spirit, who blesses spontaneously. Religion is slow and lethargic. The Holy Spirit is quick and powerful.

Religion is continually critical. The Holy Spirit is patient and helpful, understanding our weaknesses (Rom. 8:26). Religion is cold as ice and never nice. The Spirit of the living God is full of fire to awaken our desires (Luke 3:16).

> The kingdom of God is not in word but in power.
> —1 Corinthians 4:20

Sadly, most traditional churches do not operate in the power of the Holy Spirit. That is why people tend to fall asleep or do not even bother to attend their services. Where God is, there is love, unity, and a display

Introduction

of the supernatural. (See 1 Corinthians 12:28; Psalm 133; James 3:16.)

The only reason I know the Bible is that I had two supernatural experiences with my Creator in January 1990. Before that, I had consistently attended the traditional church services as a child, but I struggled to stay awake as I found it extremely boring. I realize that churches differ based on the pastor or priest presiding (this was certainly true for the lively Church of England in Brunei where I ministered), but church people typically reflect the life (or lack thereof) of their leader (Hos. 4:9). I am thankful that the churches I attended during my youth sustained me until the Holy Spirit came in to awaken my spirit to true spiritual vitality.

If any of the denominational founders were alive today, I do not think many of them would attend their own churches, because they have camped on one basic truth, salvation by grace through faith, but have not progressed forward into the fullness of the blessing of Christ (Rom. 15:19, 29). During the Dark Ages, Luther's revelation was revolutionary, and that heavenly truth still is today. Yet it is only part of the gospel message as more blessings are available after salvation to every believer (Heb. 6:9; John 16:12).

After God touched and visited my life, I had an awakening in which the lights were turned on, my spiritual eyes opened, my heart consumed by the fire of the Spirit, and my life immersed with the heavenly mandate. Before then, I was just your typical young man. I was a lifeguard, a fitness trainer, a little bit girl crazy, and was

God vs. Religion

busily pursuing my university degree. Thankfully, I am still childlike and playful at heart, but today I also have a spiritual hunger and divine wisdom from which I speak whenever I minister. Undoubtedly, anything I possess spiritually in love, wisdom, or power is a gift given to me by God—to Him alone be the glory.

On one of my ministry trips, a young lady from Ukraine remarked, "People who have God in their hearts are much more positive than those who don't." I agree with her. Atheists have even affirmed that this is definitely true. I know a young man who is a self-professed atheist. He commented to me that it is far better to live by absolutes than to try to please everybody and be socially correct.

While people of various religious mind-sets might say, "It's all relative," even my atheist friend realizes the necessity for a solid foundation of truth upon which to build one's life. The gospel is not an alternative but an ultimatum. Nevertheless, our loving, heavenly Father never pushes Himself on anyone. Whosoever will, can "taste and see" the Lord is good! (Ps. 34:8).

Christianity is the only world religion that believes God can live inside each of us (Col. 1:27; Rom. 8:11; John 14:16–17); speaks to us (John 10:27; 16:13; Heb. 3:7–8); and works with and through us (Mark 16:15–20; Matt. 12:28; Luke 10:17–21). I would not call Christianity a religion as much as I would call it a relationship. The sweet "still small voice" of God gently speaks to us daily if we have ears to hear and hearts to obey (1 Kings 19:12; Heb. 3:7–8). The more we heed what God is saying to us,

INTRODUCTION

the more frequently He will speak to us (Mark 4:24).

Religion loves to profit from the spiritual ignorance of people and happily takes their money. Only ignorant people buy idols—gods made with hands—that cannot hear, talk, or walk (Acts 19:24). I have traveled throughout Asia and I have seen people bow down to gods made with hands. It is both sad and hilarious to behold. It amazes me how spiritually blind people can be concerning the gods to whom they pray but from whom they hear no response.

The devil has blinded their eyes, keeping them in spiritual darkness (2 Cor. 4:4). If they are to ever get free, it will take someone to boldly cry out against their idols and show them a better way unto salvation. Sadly, many Christians are asleep in the light and are not willing to risk being publicly ridiculed. Thankfully, there are a few brave hearts filled with the Holy Spirit and boldness that refuse to tolerate this deception.

Every religion in the world prays. Christians alone, however, actually hear the voice of God to whom they pray. The risen Christ through the Holy Spirit gives His children dreams and visions, showing them "things to come" (John 16:13).

God showed me the tsunamis sweeping through Southeast Asia more than one month before they hit on December 26, 2004. I also foresaw the death of Princess Diana of Wales one month before that happened. Not fully understanding the dreams when I had them, I did not know what to do with them. Realizing that to predict such calamities would cause people to think ill of me, I decided to pray. Discovering the ways of God takes time. I frequently see people who become significant in my life in dreams before I meet them. Also, I continually have visions (while awake) concerning both my future and others to whom I minister.

Jesus is a living God! He is "the author and finisher of our faith" (Heb. 12:2). Many religious people begin their journey for truth and spirituality but usually stop somewhere along the way. They typically become disinterested because something offended them or they simply come to see that religion is not applicable to everyday life.

Truth is most attractive, but it can be offensive at times depending on which side of the fence you are on. Jesus said, "Blessed are they who are not offended in me" (Matt. 11:6, author's paraphrase). Jesus knew that He and His ministry would offend many, but the risk of offense did not slow Him down.

Origins of Religion

All religion is man-made. Religion is man's attempt to be spiritual and to access the Creator. As sincere as religion and religionists are, neither feed the spirit. If I were to take an interest in a religion other than my own, it would be Judaism, because Christ was a Jew. The roots of Christianity are in Judaism. The very fact that thirteen million Jews throughout the world are still alive, despite repeated attempts down through the ages to kill them off, attests to the sovereignty of

Introduction

God. Undoubtedly, God is still fighting for Israel, His chosen people (Exod. 14:25).

Religiosity is man-centered. Spirituality is God-centered. Religion is focused on covering and preserving self. Spirituality is enraptured with the Creator, enjoying His presence, partaking of His power, and co-laboring for His cause. To live in the Spirit, you must first die to self, which means you must relinquish control and your fixation with self.

Though God has visited my life, by no means have I attained or arrived. Yet there is one thing I do know for sure—I am now free from religion. My heart has been awakened. Therefore, I feel it is my duty to help other people get free from religion and experience God.

I want people to be themselves, express their hearts to God, and happily interact with others without the restraints of religion. I deeply desire for people to know the truth of God's Word and see the Lord as He is. I want to be a minister of the Spirit of God, through whom people may experience God in His power and see Him as He truly is.

God is all about love and grace. Religious people are quick to judge and get up in your face.

Being wicked means you have an understanding of the truth, but choose to twist and pervert it to serve your own purposes.

Religious people prefer self-righteousness, rather than submitting to God's righteousness.

Religion schools you in rules that nobody can live up to.

What Christ did on the cross at Calvary is sufficient for humanity. Religion, however, will never have tranquility because it is focused not on Christ, but on self and its inadequacy.

Unlike religion, Jesus is not interested in putting yokes on people. Jesus is in the business of removing yokes from people.

Religionists rigidly adhere to the letter of the law and are quick to condemn. Jesus is loving and gracious.

To live in the Spirit, you first must die to self. This means you must relinquish control and your fixation with self.

True spirituality is accompanied by great faith and confidence. Religion, however, is based on fear and insecurity.

Religion keeps its followers dependent and devoted through fear and ignorance.

Chapter 1

MISREPRESENTATION OF THE MASTER

RELIGION HAS ALWAYS misrepresented God's heart and personhood to humanity. Read Matthew 23 in which Jesus rebuked the Pharisees and Sadducees for perverting the ways of God with their traditions and rules. Jesus told the religionists of His day that their father was the devil (John 8:44). Jesus uttered seven judgments against the spiritually dead religious leaders of His day:

1. They teach religious rules and traditions of their own making, that do not originate from the heart or Word of God (Matt. 23:13). Jesus rebuked the religious leaders of his day for propagating adherence to the doctrines of men (Matt. 15:3, 9).

   Religious traditions suffocate people and keep them from the love and life of the Spirit, which the Creator intends for them to enjoy. Tradition makes the Word of God lose its effect upon hearts because people then cannot see past their religious rules to see the goodness of God and experience His blessings (Mark 7:13).

2. They removed the key of knowledge from the people not allowing them to enter into the kingdom of God (Matt. 23:14). The knowledge of God and His plan for salvation gives us heavenly vision and causes us to live purposefully, without which we would perish (Hos. 4:6; Prov. 29:18; 1 Tim. 2:4).

   Jesus said, "You shall know the truth, and the truth shall make you free" (John 8:32). Only the truth you know will produce freedom in your life. If you have no knowledge of the truth, you will remain in bondage. If you have a limited knowledge of truth, you will possess a limited amount of freedom. Your personal freedom is proportionate to the truth you know.

3. They would cross land and sea for a convert, after which they would, "make him twice as much a son of hell" as themselves (Matt. 23:15). That is to say they would fully entrench the person's soul in bondage and teach him to go do likewise to others. Multiplying their spiritual madness and spreading their enslavement to unsuspecting, sincere souls, they became the proselytes of hell, serving their father, the devil (John 8:44).

   One main reason the religious leaders erred spiritually was because they only knew the letter of the Word, not the Spir-

MISREPRESENTATION OF THE MASTER

it, which comes from the Author (2 Cor. 3:6). Therefore they greatly misappropriated the holy Scriptures, not knowing the heart of the Author, nor His divine power that flows from the Spirit (Matt. 22:29). To fully learn and know Scripture, you must first know the Holy Spirit, who inspired it (2 Tim. 3:16; 2 Pet. 1:20–21).

4. They broke their oaths and vows (Matt. 23:16). Though they swore and gave their word, by not keeping their word, the religious leaders proved themselves to be blind guides. "If the blind leads the blind, both will fall into a ditch" (Matt. 15:14).

5. They neglected "justice, mercy, and faith," favoring the miniscule matters of the law (Matt. 23:23). The religious teachers and Pharisees majored in the minor issues rather than focusing on the weightier matters of spirituality. Their primary motive was power and money, and they tithed the tiniest parts of their income.

6. They were more concerned with their outward appearance than the condition of their hearts (Matt. 23:25–26). Outside, they looked religious and clean, but within, they were filthy and vile. Their hearts were full of hypocrisy and wickedness (v. 28).

7. They patronize the prophets whom their forefathers killed (Matt. 23:29–30). They rejected the prophetic voices God sent to them, preferring their religion (v. 34). They preferred religious positions of prominence rather than purity of heart.

Spirituality or Religiosity?

Associating with spiritually hungry people is far more satisfying that being affiliated with any religion. Jesus said, "Seek, and you will find" (Matt. 7:7). Amazingly, the thing most religious people are truly seeking, unbeknownst to them, is a relationship with the living God. Hence, what you are seeking is seeking you.

God Himself by His Spirit puts hooks in our hearts to supernaturally draw us to Him in divine relationship (John 6:44). Thus, there is a simultaneous seeking occurring between God's Spirit and the human spirit (Rom. 8:16). Upon communing with your own heart (Ps. 4:4), and welcoming God's Holy Spirit into your heart to live and abide (Luke 11:13), your joy shall be full and your heart will overflow with the glory of your Creator.

Knowledge and wisdom are wonderful, but compared to feeling the magnificent Spirit and presence of God they are quite empty. The touch of God's Spirit is the most marvelous feeling as it fills your spirit, soul, and body. In God's presence is fullness of joy (Ps. 16:11).

I prefer feeling to philosophizing. You can philosophize all night and still feel empty. I value relationship

Misrepresentation of the Master

over religion. I believe this parallels the physical relationship between a husband and wife. If all a husband and his wife ever did was philosophize and have intellectual conversation, their connection would be limited. However, once there is affection and intimacy, their spirits, souls, and bodies will bond together and be difficult to break.

Religion prefers philosophy to relationship with the living God. Religion likes forms and methods more than seeking the Maker of heaven and Earth. Religion teaches you to discipline yourself to be a better person. Our Father in heaven touches you by His Spirit and recreates you as a new person.

****

I find Islam to be the most unattractive religion because it severely oppresses women and even other Muslims who do not embrace fanatical doctrines, traditions, and teachings. Historically, they have converted entire nations by the sword. From my travels to Muslim countries, I have found that Islam is intolerant and violent primarily because it is impotent. If you truly have something to offer people, they will take it freely without compulsion. Religion has nothing to offer people. Therefore, they have to resort to threats, intimidation, and violence to get people to comply.

Jesus took the opposite approach as He was building a spiritual kingdom within the heart of man. Jesus gave people freedom to follow Him. Jesus never pushed or manipulated people to follow Him. Not so with religion that employs every means possible to control people. True spirituality is accompanied by great faith and confidence. Religion, however, is based on fear and insecurity. It keeps its followers dependent and devoted through fear and ignorance.

*Humanity's erroneous tendency
is toward self-sufficiency.*

*Man-made religion and human effort
can never produce the glory of God.*

*Religion distracts, detours, and
dislocates us away from God.*

*Religion is merely an illusion of spirituality
and is void of any true spirituality.*

*Religion teaches you to discipline yourself to be
a better person. God in heaven touches you by
His Spirit and recreates you as a new person.*

*Most of what people are trying to accomplish
through dead religion can only be accomplished by
the working of the Spirit of God in and through you.*

Where man's ability ends, God's ability begins!

*Religion takes people deeper into bondage. The more
a person trusts in religion, the less likely they are
to enter into a relationship with the living God.*

*We need to take a second look at religion through
the light of Scripture and see it for what it truly is.*

It is not always about me, myself, and I.

Chapter 2

FIG LEAVES OF SELF-SUFFICIENCY

PEOPLE TEND TOWARD self-sufficiency. It is the natural inclination of every living thing to seek survival. But our Creator has so much more for us, more than we can ask or think (Eph. 3:20). Therefore, when we deal with our needs each day, we should involve God in the process. Our Father in heaven is an ever-present help to us at all times (Ps. 46:1). Self-sufficiency is essentially a prideful attitude that neglects God and refuses to acknowledge what He is capable of doing in our lives. God resists the proud, but gives grace to the humble.

In the beginning, Adam and Eve lived in the glory of God within the garden where all of their needs were met. It was a time and place where all that was required of them was to commune with their Creator and tend the garden. Things were rather simple until the serpent complicated matters by lying to and deceiving them.

The lie was, "You don't need God. You can be wise and be like God by getting knowledge" (Gen. 3:1–5, author's paraphrase). The reality is that knowledge apart from God is destructive and never fulfills us. Adam and Eve suddenly found this out when they disobeyed the Lord's instruction and ate of the tree of knowledge. Immediately, their eyes were opened to their nakedness as their disobedience caused God's glory to depart

FIG LEAVES OF SELF-SUFFICIENCY

from them. No longer were they covered by His glory. Instead, they were naked and ashamed.

Without the blessing and covering of their Creator, they immediately wanted to hide. To do so, they used fig leaves to wear as clothing (Gen. 3:7). Instinctively, they knew they needed a covering of some sort once the glory was removed.

It is no different today. People gravitate toward religion, because they are looking for a spiritual covering. They sense the existence of a greater glory with which to be clothed and want to get it somehow. Nevertheless, as good as their intentions may be, man-made religion and human effort can never reproduce the glory of God. In fact, it is exactly the opposite. Religion distracts, detours, and dislocates us from God. It is merely an illusion of spirituality and is devoid of any true faith or conviction.

Religion attempts to regulate and control the flesh. God takes a different approach. He touches and fills your spirit after which you do not desire the flesh. Flesh cannot conquer flesh for purposes of attaining spirituality. Only the Spirit of God can successfully crucify your fleshly desires and enable you to live in the Spirit (Rom. 8:13). Most of what people are trying to accomplish through religion can only be accomplished by the working of the Spirit of God in and through you.

> "Not by might nor by power, but by My Spirit,"
> Says the LORD of hosts.
> —ZECHARIAH 4:6

God vs. Religion

When we let go of all our anxiety and let God work, life is much sweeter. Remember, God in heaven is a Creator and He likes to intervene, orchestrate, and create opportunities for His children on Earth. It is when we come to the end of ourselves that we can begin to acknowledge and recognize our need for God. Where man's ability ends, God begins. When man trusts only in his ability, he never inwardly possesses tranquility. God enables us to have both inside and out. The Spirit of the living God strengthens us within and works through us en route to the fulfillment of our dreams.

God is a Creator. Satan is a copier.

God, by His Spirit, can be at all places, with all people, simultaneously interacting with humans throughout the world at any given time. Satan, on the other hand, is bound to one place at any given moment in time.

The Father in heaven sent His Son Jesus to die for the sins of the world and thereby redeem man from his wayward disobedience and tendency toward evil.

Jesus fully defeated Satan on the cross, regaining and reestablishing relationship with mankind by eliminating the barrier of sin through His shed blood.

There are no meaningless details in the Bible. God wants us to be discerning and fully prepared for "things to come" (John 16:13).

Our sins are as deadly as a snake. Jesus became sin for us, likening Himself unto a snake, so we could be free of sin and disease (John 3:14). When we look unto Jesus, we can look and live! Not only must we look and live, but we must also look and leave! We must see dead religion for what it is in all its deception and leave it behind.

⁂

Take a second look at religion through the light of Scripture and see it for what it truly is.

Symbols and icons have always been mistakenly worshiped and overly exalted by people.

Don't focus on God's servants and forget the Source of their power.

Faith is a fact and faith is an act— the difference is in the doing.

God is not Burger King. He does not always allow you to "Have it your way!"

Religion listens to everybody, but not God.

Many prayers are self-centered and ill-motivated.

God's thoughts are higher than ours as He is in heaven and we on Earth.

Co-labor with God for His cause and purposes in the earth, and you will not cleave to counterfeits, but be and birth originals.

When we embrace the ways of God, we can easily discern the counterfeit and cleave to the real.

To avoid deception, we must filter every experience and teaching through Scripture to ensure that it is biblical and legitimate.

Chapter 3

Satan's Counterfeits and Deceptions

God is a Creator. Satan is a copier. The living God breathes newness of life into all things. Satan is limited to his original gifting, which was to sing. That is why so much music today is corrupt with lyrics promoting premarital sex, lawlessness, murder, and death. Undoubtedly, there are wonderful songs that find their origins in the heart of man, however a sizeable portion of music today is vile and godless.

God, by His Spirit, is both omnipresent and omnipotent. God can simultaneously interact with humans throughout the world at any given time. Satan, on the other hand, is bound to one place at any given moment. Lucifer, as he was formerly called, was originally the archangel who led worship and praise in heaven before the throne of God (Ezek. 28:13–19).

Caught in the snare of pride, Lucifer sought to establish himself above the Most High God. Almighty God immediately dealt with this rebellion and removed the archangel from his position along with the one-third of the angels who followed him (Isa. 14:12–15; Rev. 12:4). Satan, as he is now called, primarily moves through his fallen angels. The angels who followed him are now working as demonic spirits to thwart the plan of God for humanity.

Since Satan desperately desires to get back at God, he is determined to trouble and deceive humanity, the apple of God's eye. In hindering God's plan for man, Satan seeks to reassert himself and establish his own kingdom in authority.

****

God, in His great omniscience, foresaw the cunning devices of Satan. The Father in heaven sent His Son Jesus to die for the sins of the world and thereby redeem man from his wayward disobedience. Jesus ultimately and fully defeated Satan on the cross, regaining and reestablishing relationship with mankind by eliminating the barrier of sin through His shed blood.

There is no originality in the heart of the devil as he was created and has a beginning and end. Therefore, his existence is limited. One counterfeit of Satan is his version of the Trinity. The Godhead consists of the Father, the Son, and the Holy Spirit. Satan's hierarchy consists of the devil, the false prophet, and the Antichrist, which comprise the unholy trinity (Rev. 16:13).

God in heaven became an incarnate man when He sent His Son Jesus to Earth through the womb of a virgin. The devil also became incarnate when he entered the serpent in the Garden of Eden and the heart of Judas. Through the coming Antichrist, Satan will be fully incarnate in flesh and blood.

****

Satan's Counterfeits and Deceptions

There are no meaningless details in the Bible. God does not tell us things to scare us, but to help us be discerning and fully prepared for what is ahead. It is the Father's desire to always show His children the "things to come" (John 16:13). God wants us to be prepared and alert, as He knows the devil seeks to devour and destroy us (John 10:10).

Thankfully, we have the greater power inside of us in the inward-abiding Holy Spirit, by which we can conquer all demonic forces in the name of Jesus (Luke 10:17–21). Therefore, we have nothing to fear because, "Greater is He that is in us than that which is in the world" opposing us at any given time (1 John 4:4).

The pity is when humanity falls for religion—hook, line, and sinker. Just as a fish nibbles on a lure, thinking it is food, so do many feed on religion, expecting to be nourished. Religion contaminates the soul because it cannot cure nor make any whole. Engrossed in the depths of religion, many adhere closely to its rules. Religion takes people who think they are on course for a personal breakthrough deeper into bondage. The more a person trusts in religion, the less likely they are to enter into a relationship with the living God.

When we look unto Jesus, the Author and Finisher of our faith, we can live. The children of Israel were bitten by snakes in the wilderness when they sinned against God (Num. 21:4–7). When Moses prayed to the Lord for them, God instructed Moses to put a snake on a pole and lift it up. He told the people who were ill to look at the snake on the pole and they would live (vv.

God vs. Religion

8–9). The snake on a pole is known as Caduceus and is used as the symbol of the medical profession, yet most people know nothing about its origin. It is a type and shadow of Christ Jesus hanging on the cross.

Our sins are as deadly as that snake. Jesus took our sin so we could be free (John 3:14). When we look to Jesus, like the people in the wilderness looked to the snake, we can look and live! Not only must we look and live (Heb. 12:2), but we must also look and leave. We must see religion for what it is in all its deception and leave it behind. When God appeared to Moses at the burning bush, Moses was amazed at the sight and looked a second time (Exod. 3:2–3). We need to take a second look at religion through the light of Scripture and see it for what it truly is.

Symbols and icons have always been mistakenly worshiped and overly exalted by people. The brazen serpent Moses made in the wilderness, which was a future picture of Christ lifted up on the cross, had to be destroyed by Hezekiah, because the people had begun to worship it (2 Kings 18:4). The serpent in the wilderness was not to be worshiped but looked at as a reminder of the coming Christ.

God Himself buried the bones of Moses so the people would not turn their affection toward a deceased man of God rather than God, who had called and anointed him (Deut. 34:6). How often we forget our Source and are tempted into exalting God's servants instead of honoring Him who created, called, and anointed them for divine service. Even today people overly exalt and worship the cross rather than the Christ who died upon it.

Let us not place our affection on the cross rather than on Christ, who died for us. People often misplace their affection on things that cannot fill or satisfy the soul. Then, when nothing happens in their life as expected, they often get angry at God when it is not God's fault. Our Creator has outlined in His Word the parameters and means by which He moves. Most however do not take the interest or invest the time to read the Bible so as to learn the ways of God.

The children of Israel only knew God's acts, whereas Moses knew His ways (Ps. 103:7). When you know the ways of God, you can cooperate and co-labor with Him to do His mighty acts!

****

God has bound Himself to His Word, which He honors above His name (Ps. 138:2). When you execute God's Word and move upon it with childlike faith, the Father in heaven will faithfully perform it in your life. The God of heaven is looking for more people on Earth to take Him at His Word, which is to act unashamedly and boldly upon His Word, fully believing.

Faith is a fact and faith is an act—the difference, however, is in the doing.[1] "Faith without works is dead" (James 2:26). It is time we put feet to our faith and let God arise in our midst. When we do, God will give us the victory and cause our enemies to be scattered.

God vs. Religion

Self-Exaltation, Religious Deviation

We must remember that God is not Burger King. He does not always allow you to "Have it your way!" He is the King of kings, ruling and reigning over the earth. God does it His way and unless you learn and discover His ways, you will not get very far with Him, no matter how much you pray.

If we regard iniquity in our hearts, the Lord will not hear us (Ps. 66:18). This means the Lord does not respond to sinful, unrepentant hearts; our sins can separate us from God (Isa. 59:2). Many prayers are self-centered and ill-motivated, just as religion is self-centered.

No spiritual reasons for Lucifer's departure were given other than "I will," "I want," and "I am" (Isa. 14:12–15). When Jesus taught us how to pray, He began by focusing on the Father, the Father's kingdom, and the Father's will (Matt. 6:9–13). Satanic religion as clearly stated in the satanic Bible begins by saying, "Satan represents indulgence instead of abstinence."[1] The devil basically is saying, "Do whatever you want."

****

We must pray with the heart of God in mind, fully considering His will and ways. It is not always about me, myself, and I. God's thoughts are higher than ours as He is in heaven and we are on Earth.

We must endeavor to know God. Let go of earthly things that can never satisfy and place them in their

Satan's Counterfeits and Deceptions

proper perspective. Co-laboring with God for His cause and purpose in the earth means you will not cleave to counterfeits. When we embrace the ways of God we can easily discern the counterfeit and cleave to the real. We can look and live. We can feel and heal. We can arise to be all God wants us to be. With God as our Friend, our ears will hear and our eyes will see.

The Bible boldly and clearly identifies falsehood throughout the sacred text. Here are some examples:

- A false matter (Exod. 23:7)
- A false report (Exod. 23:1)
- A false witness (Exod. 20:16; Deut. 5:20; 19:16; Prov. 6:19; 19:5, 9)
- Swearing falsely (Lev. 6:3–5; Jer. 5:2; Mal. 3:5)
- Dealing falsely (Lev. 19:11; Jer. 6:13; 8:10)
- Swearing by God's Name falsely (Lev. 19:12; Zech. 5:4)
- A false testimony (Deut. 19:18; Jer. 40:16)
- Answering falsely (Job 21:34)
- False words (Job 36:4; Isa. 32:7; 59:13)
- Conceiving falsehood (Ps. 7:14)
- Dealing falsely with covenant (Ps. 44:17; Hos. 10:4)

God vs. Religion

- False ways (Ps. 119:104, 128)
- Deceptive disobedience leading to falsehood (Ps. 119:118)
- A false tongue (Ps. 109:2; 120:3; Prov. 6:17)
- Vain mouths with falsehood in their hands (Ps. 144:8, 11)
- A false balance (Prov. 11:1; 20:23)
- False lips (Ps. 31:18; 120:2; Prov. 17:4; Matt. 5:11)
- A false gift (Prov. 25:14; Acts 8:20; 16:16)
- A false covenant (Isa. 28:15)
- Children, a seed, of falsehood (Isa. 30:9; 57:4)
- Prophesy falsely (Jer. 5:31; 29:9)
- False ministry operations (Jer. 6:13)
- False gods and images (Jer. 10:14; 51:17)
- False trust (Jer. 13:25)
- A false vision and divination (Jer. 14:14; Ezek. 21:23; Acts 16:16)
- False dreams (Jer. 23:32; Zech. 10:2)
- False accusation (Jer. 37:13-15; Luke 19:8; 2 Tim. 3:3; Rev. 12:10)
- False burdens and causes (Lam. 2:14)

Satan's Counterfeits and Deceptions

- Commit falsehood, opening the door to thievery (Hos. 7:1)

- The spirit of falsehood (Mic. 2:11; 2 Chron. 18:20–22)

- Lying vanities (Jon. 2:8; Ps. 31:6)

- False oaths (Zech. 8:17)

- False prophets (Matt. 7:15; 24:11; Luke 6:26; Acts 13:6)

- False christs (Mark 13:22)

- False apostles (2 Cor. 11:13)

- False brethren (2 Cor. 11:26; Gal. 2:4)

- False signs and wonders that are a lie (2 Thess. 2:9)

- False knowledge and science (1 Tim. 6:20)

- False teachers (2 Pet. 2:1)

- Lying falsely against the Lord (Isa. 59:13)

God vs. Religion

Religious Deception

Let go of counterfeits
Forget the religious show
Enter the realm of the Spirit
Enter the divine flow
For there you will know
There you will see.
There you will find and experience
Perfect liberty
Internal tranquility
Delightful harmony
Rid yourself of distasteful religion
Remember its origin
That it comes from man
Mean business with God
For there is a new and living way
For you today!
Jesus is the Way
He is the Truth and Life
So stop quarreling about religion
Rid your soul of strife
Knowledge never satisfies
Apart from the Spirit
It just intensifies your confusion
While adding to the illusion
Keeping you ignorant and bound
In it no life is found
It has no liberating sound
Just a confining whisper
A "Shhh!" to keep you quiet

Satan's Counterfeits and Deceptions

I say forget dead religion!
Let's start a riot
A riot of righteousness
To free all the captives
To open the prisons
Prisons with stained glass windows
Holding all the saintly seekers
Who have the look of religion
Without the power to keep you
A new day do I declare
For whosoever will
Jesus opened the prison doors
So you can be set free
Discern the difference
Between religiosity and reality
Between liturgy and true spirituality
Between tradition and transformation
Between information and inspiration
Between formality and the force of faith
Between "someday" and this day
Jesus is the great I AM
Meaning today is the day to celebrate
To get real
To listen to your heart
And truly feel
To awake to the Spirit
To move in the Spirit
To abandon dead religion
And the entanglements near it
Freedom is yours
Cherish it every day

God vs. Religion

For many are they
Who don't know the way
For those who remain
In the depths of religious bondage
Desiring more
But still unsure
Undecided and uncommitted
To discover the way
Unwilling to read the Bible
For themselves today
So laziness and ignorance
Will keep them impoverished
Though the external
Looks nice and polished
Within they are dying
Drying up inside
If only
They would awake and realize
God has so much more
So much better
Yet they cleave to counterfeits
Like dry old leather
Would somebody please
Lift up their voice
Show them there is more
Tell them their life
Need not be such a bore.
Before it's all over
All will at least hear
Yet whether or not they understand
Remains to be seen

Satan's Counterfeits and Deceptions

> Because the religion that holds them
> Appears nice but it is mean
> Not everything my friend
> Is as what it seems.

I remember comedian Steve Martin's movie *Leap of Faith*, in which he depicts a traveling evangelist. He portrayed a minister as a charlatan, and did not cast the pastorate in a good light. His character was very showy and flashy, unlike most ministers I know. Martin actually followed Pastor Benny Hinn around to prepare for his role. I attended Pastor Hinn's church for two-and-a-half years, and I can honestly say that what he has is from God and is authentic, which was not the case with the character in Martin's movie. It made me realize that the counterfeit often tries to belittle the real and legitimate in an attempt to exalt itself instead.

****

To avoid deception, we must filter every experience and teaching through Scripture to ensure that it is biblical and legitimate. The Holy Bible has much to say about truth and lies, real and false, and good and evil. A counterfeit that deceives and causes people to put trust in that which is unable to produce in their lives is most wicked and evil.

*Ignorance is an open door for religion
to come in and deceive you.*

*People perish and go to hell for
ignorance and lack of knowledge.*

*The ignorant are both proud of and
blind to their current condition.*

*Religion betrays with a tender kiss outwardly,
while it continues to hiss inwardly until
the opportune time comes to slay you.*

*Religion deceives by saying one
thing and delivering another.*

*Look for authenticity and spirituality
rather than religion.*

*If it does not feel right in your gut, then
you may be entering a religious rut.*

*Before diving headfirst into a shallow pool of
religion, people should carefully and prayerfully
consider what they are getting into.*

Chapter 4

IGNORANCE IS NOT BLISS

THE OLD EXPRESSION "ignorance is bliss" could not be further from the truth. Ignorance is an open door for deception to come in and destroy you. People perish and go to hell for lack of knowledge as God clearly says in Hosea 4:6: "My people are destroyed for lack of knowledge." The mouth of hell is wide open and ready to receive people who believe a lie, trust in religion instead of a relationship with their Creator, and refuse the truth of God's Word (Isa. 5:13).

Ironically, people who are ignorant do not know they are, for they lack the knowledge that could help them. Most are blind and clueless as to their present condition. Therefore, the devil is lurking in the shadows, waiting for an opportune time to strike and devour them.

Ignorance is an open door through which religion enters to deceive you. The serpent in the garden appeared as Eve's friend, talking like he had her best interest at heart. Judas, who betrayed Jesus, did so with a kiss, as if he were greatly affectionate toward Jesus (Mark 14:44). The adulteress in the Bible went to church and paid her vows (Prov. 7:14), but the minute her husband was away, she dove into the bed with another man.

****

God vs. Religion

When I was in India, I went to a restaurant in Bangalore that appeared to have a very impressive menu. The dishes looked extraordinary and seemed to have very generous portions. One sandwich was described as having "mounds of thick roast beef." The picture next to the description looked just like one back home at an American deli. I ordered the sandwich, and when it arrived, it consisted mostly of bread, a few very small pieces of diced roast beef, a lot of mayonnaise and mustard, some wilted lettuce, and a pitiful tomato wedge. Immediately, I complained, saying, "This is *not* what the menu says! You have deceived me!"

Religion is no different. It deceives people by saying one thing and delivering another. People deceived by religion go to church expecting and needing one thing but wind up getting something completely different. I could have been happy going home and making myself a sandwich instead of eating at that horrible, deceiving restaurant where I had to pay for that horrid sandwich. The menu should have read, "Mustard, mayonnaise, wilted lettuce, and rotten little tomato sandwich with a few tiny pieces of roast beef."

If the marquee outside religious edifices would only tell us what we are truly getting, or not getting, inside, it would save us all a lot of time and trouble. Perhaps a marquee that read, "Religion: lots of liturgy, an opportunity to give an offering, and a quiet place to sleep" would be more appropriate.

****

IGNORANCE IS NOT BLISS

Fraudulent representations, in which you wrongly assume and expect something, occur every day. The world in which we live can be a cruel and merciless place. Greedy people and companies, who are only out to make a quick buck, surround us. We must be very discerning and alert. We do not want counterfeits. However, to quickly recognize imitations and misrepresentations, we must first know the true and legitimate.

Bank employees are trained to handle genuine currency, so when fraudulent bills arrive, they can quickly recognize them. When you give a hundred dollar bill to a local grocer or convenience store clerk, you may see them mark it with a special marker to inspect its authenticity. Likewise, we should test religion for authenticity and spirituality against our Spirit-guided discernment. If it does not feel right in your gut, you may be entering a religious rut. Before diving headfirst into a shallow pool of religion, people should carefully and prayerfully consider what they are getting into.

∞

Hypocrites hide behind religious masks and speech.

Religion toils tirelessly to compete with spirituality, but always comes up short and shallow.

There is no grace or elegance in religion—only rude religious leaders, rules, and an unscriptural opinion.

Religion condemns, controls, and contains.

Religion ridicules and disdains. God loves everyone the same.

Religionists build and take ownership of denominations. God has no earthly alliances or affiliations.

Religionists are self-righteous and outwardly pious. God's kids find their sufficiency in Him and always win.

Religionists pray so that they can be heard and esteemed by men. Believers pray because they have an eternal Friend.

A council and committee cannot slow down God, but it sure can make Him want to move to a church down the street where they believe, obey, and applaud.

Chapter 5

Mouth Traps

If I were to choose two animals that best describe religion, they would be a peacock and a hyena. The peacock parades about and the hyena is a scavenger, living off the life of others. Hyenas have powerful jaws but are quite ugly creatures. They have a hideous squeal and demonic-like laugh. They remind me of the self-righteous religious rulers who condemned the adulterous woman in the Bible. They are the ones who told blind Bartimaeus to shut up when he was crying out for Jesus. The parading Pharisees of Jesus' day, who were quick to snarl and ridicule, epitomize religion.

Religious leaders have always opposed moves of God and spiritual men who have led them, because they want to maintain control over people and keep their hands in others' pocketbooks. Religion is money and ego driven, not God inspired. That is why the ruthless religious rulers were pushy and intrusive when it came time to collect and count the tithe (Matt. 23:23).

Subtle and Sly Religionists

Religious people will tell you one thing, but while they speak, you will inwardly sense another. It is like they are out to get you, but gloss it over with sweet, religious verbiage.

God vs. Religion

The religious rulers secretly waited for Jesus, seeking to trap Him into saying something with which they might be able to accuse Him (Luke 11:54). Jesus often discerned the thoughts or line of reasoning by which the rulers worked (Matt. 22:18; Mark 2:8; Luke 5:22).

A demon-possessed woman met the apostle Paul and his men as they were heading to a place of prayer. She said all the right things, but was manifesting a devil (Acts 16:16–17). The devil is very subtle and sly, not unlike some religious people. No wonder the devil chose to come through the serpent in the Garden of Eden.

Unbeknownst to most, the devil does attend church (Mark 1:23–26). Jesus did not hesitate to cast out a devil at the synagogue whenever they showed up. Evil spirits like to infiltrate and infest human souls. Demons often use people to exert their influence and control over others. The devil rarely uses strangers to get to you. Satan likes to use people you know to influence you. That is why Scripture says we do not wrestle against flesh and blood, but against spiritual wickedness (Eph. 6:12).

David, a man after God's own heart, acknowledged his enemies' subtleties: "The words of his mouth were smoother than butter, but war was in his heart; His words were softer than oil, yet they were drawn swords" (Ps. 55:21). Religion toils tirelessly to compete with spirituality, but always comes up short and shallow. Every critical word religion speaks against spirituality only serves to identify religion's stupidity and inferiority. Empty barrels always make the most noise. "The words of a wise man's mouth are gracious, but the lips of a fool shall swallow him up" (Eccles. 10:12).

There is no grace or elegance in religion, only insensitive religious leaders, rules, and unscriptural opinion. Jesus did not quarrel, cry out, or lift His voice in the streets (Matt. 12:19). Everyone bore witness of Jesus and wondered at the gracious words that proceeded out of His mouth (Luke 4:22). The majority of Jesus' enemies were religious people or the few in political power who felt threatened by His influence. Their lying accusations and threats were the primary avenue of attack against Jesus. God reveals in His Word that all our enemies will eventually open their mouths against us (Lam. 3:46). They will "hiss and gnash their teeth" (Lam. 2:16). Their tongues are like arrows shot out, speaking peaceably to deceive while harboring malice within (Jer. 9:8).

Religious Councils Conspiring and Killing

Religious people sometimes try to be quite clever and maneuver to thwart what God is doing by His Spirit. What's funny, however, is that God is always one step ahead of them, and He is continuously revealing to His people what they are up to.

Religious people make strange alliances to accomplish their anti-Christ purposes. "The Pharisees... plotted with the Herodians against Him [Christ], how they might destroy Him" (Mark 3:6). The Pharisees took counsel how they might entangle Jesus in his talk (Matt. 22:15). All the chief priests and elders of the people took counsel against Jesus to put him to death

God vs. Religion

(Matt. 27:1). If religion cannot control you, it will seek to kill you. The religious rulers would do anything to rid Jesus of His influence over the people. These religionists were insanely jealous and controlling. When Jesus refused to succumb to their control, they did not hesitate to try to kill Him.

> But the angel answered and said to the women, "Do not be afraid, for I know that you seek Jesus who was crucified. He is not here; for He is risen, as He said. Come, see the place where the Lord lay. And go quickly and tell His disciples that He is risen from the dead, and indeed He is going before you into Galilee; there you will see Him. Behold, I have told you." So they went out quickly from the tomb with fear and great joy, and ran to bring His disciples word. And as they went to tell His disciples, behold, Jesus met them, saying, "Rejoice!" So they came and held Him by the feet and worshiped Him. Then Jesus said to them, "Do not be afraid. Go and tell My brethren to go to Galilee, and there they will see Me." Now while they were going, behold, some of the guard came into the city and reported to the chief priests all the things that had happened. When they had assembled with the elders and consulted together, they gave a large sum of money to the soldiers, saying, "Tell them, 'His disciples came at night and stole Him away while we slept.' And if this comes to the governor's ears, we will appease him and make you secure." So they took the money and did as they

were instructed; and this saying is commonly reported among the Jews until this day.
—MATTHEW 28:5–15

Men of Israel, hear these words: Jesus of Nazareth, a Man attested by God to you by miracles, wonders, and signs which God did through Him in your midst, as you yourselves also know—Him, being delivered by the determined purpose and foreknowledge of God, you have taken by lawless hands, have crucified, and put to death; whom God raised up, having loosed the pains of death, because it was not possible that He should be held by it.
—ACTS 2:22–24

Overthrowing Religion With Holy Spirit Dominion

Now as they spoke to the people, the priests, the captain of the temple, and the Sadducees came upon them, being greatly disturbed that they taught the people and preached in Jesus the resurrection from the dead. And they laid hands on them, and put them in custody until the next day, for it was already evening. However, many of those who heard the word believed; and the number of the men came to be about five thousand. And it came to pass, on the next day, that their rulers, elders, and scribes, as well as Annas the high priest, Caiaphas, John, and Alexander, and as many as were of the family of the high priest, were gathered together at Jerusalem. And when they had set them in the midst, they asked, "By what power or by what name have you done this?" Then Peter, filled with the Holy Spirit, said to them, "Rulers of the people and elders of Israel: If we this day are judged for a good deed done to a helpless man, by what means he has been made well, let it be known to you all, and to all the people of Israel, that by the name of Jesus Christ of Nazareth, whom you crucified, whom God raised from the dead, by Him this man stands here before you whole. This is the 'stone which was rejected by you builders, which has become the chief cornerstone.' Nor is there salvation in any other, for there is no other name under heaven given among men by which we must be saved."

Now when they saw the boldness of Peter and John, and perceived that they were uneducated and untrained men, they marveled. And they realized that they had been with Jesus. And seeing the man who had been healed standing with them, they could say nothing against it.

But when they had commanded them to go aside out of the council, they conferred among themselves, saying, "What shall we do to these men? For, indeed, that a notable miracle has been done through them is evident to all who dwell in Jerusalem, and we cannot deny it. But so that it spreads no further among the people, let us severely threaten them, that from now on they speak to no man in this name." So they called them and commanded them not to speak at all nor teach in the name of Jesus. But Peter and John answered and said to them, "Whether it is right in the sight of God to listen to you more than to God, you judge. For we cannot but speak the things which we have seen and heard." So when they had further threatened them, they let them go, finding no way of punishing them, because of the people, since they all glorified God for what had been done.

—Acts 4:1–21

When God confirms His Word with power through His servants, religion applies pressure to try to control them. God helps and heals people. Religion hurts and harasses people. Peter said, "We are His witnesses to these things, and so also is the Holy Spirit whom God has given to those who obey Him. When they heard this, they were furious and plotted to kill them" (Acts 5:32–33). Religionists are cowards. God's men are Christlike and courageous. Religion likes to control. God wants to make you whole.

> But Saul increased all the more in strength, and confounded the Jews who dwelt in Damascus, proving that this Jesus is the Christ. Now after many days were past, the Jews plotted to kill him.
>
> —Acts 9:22–23

Religion prefers, produces, and preys on spiritual weakness. God fills you with supernatural strength.

God vs. Religion

Religion controls and kills. Jesus liberates and gives abundant life. Religious people are big talkers, which I believe further confirms their deception. Excessive verbiage nullifies one's religion and exposes one's vanity:

> If anyone among you thinks he is religious, and does not bridle his tongue but deceives his own heart, this one's religion is useless.
> —James 1:26

> You are snared by the words of your mouth; You are taken by the words of your mouth.
> —Proverbs 6:2

> The mouth of the foolish is near destruction.
> —Proverbs 10:14

> The hypocrite with his mouth destroys his neighbor.
> —Proverbs 11:9

> Whoever guards his mouth and tongue keeps his soul from troubles.
> —Proverbs 21:23

> A lying tongue hates those who are crushed by it, and a flattering mouth works ruin.
> —Proverbs 26:28

Christ was constantly oppressed and afflicted until His crucifixion. Yet He did not open His mouth. He was brought, "as a lamb to the slaughter, and as a sheep before its shearers is silent, so He opened not His mouth" (Isa. 53:7).

Jesus "made His grave with the wicked—but with the rich at His death, because He had done no violence, nor was any deceit in His mouth" (Isa. 53:9). Religion often slays the innocent. Rome not only killed Jesus, but also many more innocent believers in Christ during the Inquisition. Religion is boastful and boisterous, whereas Christ is confident and abides in quietness. By our own words, we will be justified and condemned. Jesus, therefore, wisely is quick to hear and slow to speak.

Religious people seem to master the art of giving lip service while removing their hearts far from God. Jesus and Isaiah both acknowledged a people who drew near to God with their mouths, and honored Him with their lips; but their hearts were far from Him (Matt. 15:8). Jesus boldly rebuked them saying, "Brood of vipers! How can you, being evil, speak good things? For out of the abundance of the heart the mouth speaks" (Matt. 12:34). Your mouth is the biggest danger to the direction of your life, which is steered by the words of your mouth. God exhorts us not to allow our mouths to cause our flesh to sin (Eccles. 5:6).

Religious Leaders Under Judgment

Religious overseers sometimes have ill intentions and oppress God's people. The chief Shepherd, Jesus, does not tolerate spiritual abuse and quickly comes to rescue His people from the snares of the masters of religion:

> Thus says the Lord God: "Behold, I am against the shepherds, and I will require My flock at their

God vs. Religion

> hand; I will cause them to cease feeding the sheep, and the shepherds shall feed themselves no more; for I will deliver My flock from their mouths, that they may no longer be food for them."
> —Ezekiel 34:10

Not every word that comes out of the mouth of a religious leader is to be trusted. Like the believers in Berea, we must earnestly search Scripture and verify that what is being taught is accurate and biblically based (Acts 17:10–11).

> Thus says the Lord of hosts: "Do not listen to the words of the prophets who prophesy to you. They make you worthless; they speak a vision of their own heart, not from the mouth of the Lord."
> —Jeremiah 23:16

The devil knows the Word of God more than most Christians. Satan quoted Scripture to Jesus (Matt. 4:5–6), though it was out of context and far removed from the heart of God. Nevertheless, he was knowledgeable of the Word. It is dangerous when the devil knows the Bible better than most Christians. We must know the Word in spirit and truth, lest we be deceived in these last days.

> My people are destroyed for lack of knowledge. Because you have rejected knowledge, I also will reject you from being [a] priest for me.
> —Hosea 4:6

> Therefore Sheol [hell] has enlarged itself and opened its mouth beyond measure; their glory

and their multitude and their pomp, and he who is jubilant, shall descend into it.
> —Isaiah 5:14

If we will have ears to hear, Jesus will speak to us through the Holy Spirit. Jesus said His sheep would hear His voice (John 10:27). It is the word within the mouth of God that has the most bearing and final authority.

> Let God be true but every man a liar.
> —Romans 3:4

> While the word was still in the king's mouth, a voice fell from heaven: "King Nebuchadnezzar, to you it is spoken: the kingdom has departed from you!"
> —Daniel 4:31

Many are speaking, but few say anything worth listening to. Regarding the others, we should pray that God would shut their mouths and silence them. God is in the business of both opening mouths filled with His Word (Ps. 81:10), and shutting mouths of those who oppose His will.

> My God sent His angel and shut the lions' mouths, so that they have not hurt me, because I was found innocent before Him; and also, O king, I have done no wrong before you.
> —Daniel 6:22

> And the angel answered and said to him, "I am Gabriel, who stands in the presence of God, and

> was sent to speak to you and bring you these glad tidings. But behold, you will be mute and not able to speak until the day these things take place, because you did not believe my words which will be fulfilled in their own time."
>
> —LUKE 1:19–20

We do not have to fear because our God will fight for us. We never need to lie to protect ourselves (Zeph. 3:13). God wants us to stand strong and separate the precious from the vile. The Lord of glory is looking for people to be His mouth in the earth (Jer. 15:19). The rebellious in the land are many. Nevertheless, God wants us to honor Him and open our mouths to speak His truth in this hour (Ezek. 2:8).

Hardheaded and Hardhearted

We must eat what God gives us from His Word and open our mouths boldly to speak what He tells us. Many times, it is the people most familiar with us who are quickest to reject the message God gives us. Nevertheless, we are to be strong and not yield to their hardheartedness (Ezek. 3:1–7).

> I have made your face strong against their faces, and your forehead strong against their foreheads. Like adamant stone, harder than flint, I have made your forehead; do not be afraid of them, nor be dismayed at their looks, though they are a rebellious house.
>
> —EZEKIEL 3:8–9

Mouth Traps

The Lord put forth His hand and touched my mouth, and the Lord said to me: "Behold, I have put My words in your mouth."

—Jeremiah 1:9

Because you speak this word, behold, I will make My words in your mouth fire, and this people wood.

—Jeremiah 5:14

For the word of God is living and powerful, and sharper than any two-edged sword.

—Hebrews 4:12

In the shadow of His hand He has hidden me, and made me a polished shaft.

—Isaiah 49:2

My word that goes forth from My mouth; It shall not return to me void, but it shall accomplish what I please, and it shall prosper in the thing for which I sent it.

—Isaiah 55:11

"My covenant with them: My Spirit who is upon you, and My words which I have put in your mouth, shall not depart from your mouth, nor from the mouth of your descendants, nor from the mouth of your descendants' descendants," says the Lord, "from this time and forevermore."

—Isaiah 59:21

Despite religious mouth traps, our God shall be mighty to attract a holy people unto Himself, through whom He can fill the earth with His Word and Spirit. God's people shall not be ashamed. The Lord of glory will bless His people and their seed forevermore. All generations shall rejoice in the Lord their Maker! For God Most High is a religious bondage breaker. The words that proceed from God's mouth and servants are forever true. Christ has done it all; there is nothing left to do. Now it is time to arise and declare the truth because His Spirit is upon you.

God does not promise loaves to spiritual loafers.

Religion lures souls with presents.

Religion takes vows of poverty and encourages peasantry. God's presence brings prosperity.

Selfish souls seek the gifts but forget the Giver.

In God's eyes, you are the greatest gift.

Where there are presents, there is impatience. Where God's presence is, there is divine essence.

Present yourself to God in all your insufficiency and inability. He will wholeheartedly embrace you with His loving presence.

Religion needs costly robes and gaiety to dress it up. The presence of God needs no outward adorning to lift you up.

Where there are gifts among people, there comparison will be found. Where God's presence is, love will abound.

Chapter 6

Presents Versus Presence

Like Abraham, our father of faith, we too must continually lift up our hands to heaven for supply. As we do we make it known in heaven and Earth that God above is our Source. Jesus clearly stated that man will serve either God or money, but cannot serve both (Matt. 6:24). This world pulls upon us to be motivated by money. Such temptation is common to ministers as well:

> Now the king of Sodom said to Abram, "Give me the persons, and take the goods for yourself." But Abram said to the king of Sodom, "I have raised my hand to the Lord, God Most High, the Possessor of heaven and earth, that I will take nothing, from a thread to a sandal strap, and that I will not take anything that is yours, lest you should say, 'I have made Abram rich.'"
>
> —Genesis 14:21–23

> In Your presence is fullness of joy; at Your right hand are pleasures forevermore.
>
> —Psalm 16:11

> Gehazi, the servant of Elisha the man of God, said, "Look, my master has spared Naaman this Syrian, while not receiving from his hands what

Presents Versus Presence

> he brought; but as the LORD lives, I will run after him and take something from him."
>
> —2 KINGS 5:20

> Now he went in and stood before his master. Elisha said to him, "Where did you go, Gehazi?" And he said, "Your servant did not go anywhere." Then he said to him, "Did not my heart go with you when the man turned back from his chariot to meet you? Is it time to receive money and to receive clothing, olive groves and vineyards, sheep and oxen, male and female servants? Therefore the leprosy of Naaman shall cling to you and your descendants forever." And he went out from his presence leprous, as white as snow.
>
> —2 KINGS 5:25–27

It was not the time to receive gifts. Elisha had carefully instructed that no gifts were to be received from Naaman, however Gehazi's covetous heart got the best of him and led him astray.

Obedience Is Better Than Sacrifice

It is better to possess your soul than to be possessed by possessions. Obedience is better than sacrifice. The Spirit of the Lord departed from Saul because of his disobedience, after which an evil spirit from the Lord troubled him (1 Sam. 16:14).

The prophet Samuel asked Saul:

> "Why then did you not obey the voice of the LORD? Why did you swoop down on the spoil,

and do evil in the sight of the Lord?" And Saul said to Samuel, "But I have obeyed the voice of the Lord, and gone on the mission on which the Lord sent me, and brought back Agag king of Amalek; I have utterly destroyed the Amalekites. But the people took of the plunder, sheep and oxen, the best of the things which should have been utterly destroyed, to sacrifice to the Lord your God in Gilgal." So Samuel said: "Has the Lord as great delight in burnt offerings and sacrifices, as in obeying the voice of the Lord? Behold, to obey is better than sacrifice, and to heed than the fat of rams. For rebellion is as the sin of witchcraft, and stubbornness is as iniquity and idolatry. Because you have rejected the word of the Lord, He also has rejected you from being king." Then Saul said to Samuel, "I have sinned, for I have transgressed the commandment of the Lord and your words, because I feared the people and obeyed their voice."

—1 Samuel 15:19–24

Sometimes, both with God and men, no recompense will be accepted, even if we try to appease with many gifts (Prov. 6:35). Undoubtedly, positions of power and the giving of gifts make many friends, but some things matter more than money. God let His people become defiled through their gifts—the sacrifice of every firstborn—that He might fill them with horror so they would know that He is the Lord (Ezek. 20:26). The Lord was so enraged by His people who were sacrificing their sons in the fire and defiling themselves with

Presents Versus Presence

all their idols that He refused to answer them when they inquired of Him (Ezek. 20:31).

> "As for you, O house of Israel," thus says the Lord God: "Go, serve every one of you his idols—and hereafter—if you will not obey Me; but profane My holy name no more with your gifts and your idols…And there you shall remember your ways and all your doings with which you were defiled; and you shall loathe yourselves in your own sight because of all the evils that you have committed."
> —Ezekiel 20:39, 43

Daniel was a man of God who could not be bought. Belshazzar, the king, heard that Daniel could make interpretations and dissolve doubts, so he said:

> "Now if you can read the writing and make known to me its interpretation, you shall be clothed with purple and have a chain of gold around your neck, and shall be the third ruler in the kingdom." Then Daniel answered, and said before the king, "Let your gifts be for yourself, and give your rewards to another; yet I will read the writing to the king, and make known to him the interpretation."
> —Daniel 5:16–17

Love, Thanksgiving, and Rejoicing

God encourages us in His Word to earnestly covet the best gifts. Yet He also shows us a better way (1 Cor. 12:31). This is the way of love.

God vs. Religion

The Pharisees were loveless leaders, stuck on religious duties and practices. Jesus rebuked them, saying, "But woe to you Pharisees! For you tithe mint and rue and all manner of herbs, and pass by justice and the love of God. These you ought to have done, without leaving the others undone" (Luke 11:42).

Jesus freely gave ministry gifts to His church in order to perfect us for the work of the ministry and to edify us in love. His plan is to bring us all into the unity of the faith and the knowledge of the Son of God; to bring us unto a perfect Man, unto the measure of the stature of the fullness of Christ (Eph. 4:8, 11–13).

The gifts of religion are sold to raise money. "How shall we escape if we neglect so great a salvation?" (Heb. 2:3). Perhaps we easily neglect our salvation because of the many religious distractions vying for our attention. The salvation of Christ is great and should not be neglected.

The presence of God is priceless. When we spend time with our Creator, we come out speaking with authority and glory. Our words carry weight and are full of His presence (Ps. 17:2):

> You prepare a table before me in the presence of my enemies.
>
> —Psalm 23:5

> You shall hide them in the secret place of Your presence from the plots of man; You shall keep them secretly in a pavilion from the strife of tongues.
>
> —Psalm 31:20

Presents Versus Presence

Religious people are happy to live in their own presence, but God's people want to live in God's presence. David, a man after God's own heart, fervently prayed:

> Do not cast me away from Your presence, and do not take Your Holy Spirit from me.
> —Psalm 51:11

> Let us come before His presence with thanksgiving; let us shout joyfully to Him with psalms.
> —Psalm 95:2

> The mountains melt like wax at the presence of the Lord, at the presence of the Lord of the whole earth.
> —Psalm 97:5

Whatever mountains or obstacles we face in life, when we invite God into the situation, His presence gives us the victory.

> Surely the righteous shall give thanks to Your name; the upright shall dwell in Your presence.
> —Psalm 140:13

God will not share His glory with any man or ministry. He alone is worthy of our praise and adoration. The nations need to know the presence of God. Isaiah the prophet prayed:

> Oh, that You would rend the heavens! That You would come down! That the mountains might shake at Your presence—as fire burns brushwood, as fire causes water to boil—to make

God vs. Religion

> Your name known to Your adversaries, that the nations may tremble at Your presence!
> —Isaiah 64:1–2

The presence of God shakes and awakes humanity, while also bringing down walls of division (Ezek. 38:20). Whether we ascend to the heights of heaven or make our bed in hell, there is no escaping the presence of God. Jonah tried to run from the presence of the Lord and went to Joppa. He "found a ship going to Tarshish" (Jon. 1:3). Nevertheless, God eventually won as circumstances prevailed over Jonah. A whale swallowed Jonah and spit him out into the purposes of God. No coincidence indeed. We do well to hold our peace in the presence of the Lord God, "For the day of the Lord is at hand, for the Lord has prepared a sacrifice; He has invited His guests" (Zeph. 1:7).

"There is joy in the presence of the angels of God over one sinner who repents" (Luke 15:10). Jonah repented and embraced God's presence, after which he boldly preached to Ninevah. To Jonah's surprise this wicked city repented at his preaching.

We never know how God will use us to speak to people, cities, and nations. For this reason we must always be ready and never ashamed to speak for God (2 Tim. 4:2). Jesus said, "Whoever is ashamed of Me and of My words in this adulterous and sinful generation, of him the Son of Man also will be ashamed when He comes in the glory of His Father with the holy angels" (Mark 8:38).

Presents Versus Presence

Many disciples suffer persecution and rejection for declaring the name of Jesus and His salvation to mankind. Whenever we are rejected for Christ's sake, we should embrace it wholeheartedly, realizing that we are partaking in Christ's suffering. Inasmuch as we partake in Christ's suffering, so too shall we rejoice in His glory that shall be revealed in and upon us (1 Pet. 4:13).

The apostles "departed from the presence of the council, rejoicing that they were counted worthy to suffer shame for His [Jesus'] name" (Acts 5:41). When we humble ourselves, repent, and trust in Jesus, we can be converted and have our sins blotted out. Repentance opens the way for times of refreshing to come from the presence of the Lord (Acts 3:19).

Religion is puffed up with pride, whereas, true and genuine servants of God humbly plead with your soul. The great apostle Paul considered himself to be lowly in presence. Paul pled with people by the meekness and gentleness of Christ (2 Cor. 10:1). The presence of God remains with us and enables us to work out our own salvation with fear and trembling (Phil. 2:12–13).

The apostles considered their disciples in Christ to be their hope, joy, and crown of rejoicing (1 Thess. 2:19). Unlike religion, Christ's followers find peace in His holy presence. "For Christ has not entered the holy places made with hands, which are copies of the true, but into heaven itself, now to appear in the presence of God for us" (Heb. 9:24). Jesus did "not need daily, as those high priests, to offer up sacrifice, first for His own sins and then for the people's, for this He did once for all when He offered up Himself" (Heb. 7:27).

We do not have a high priest who cannot be touched with the feeling of our infirmities. Jesus was in all points tempted like we are, yet without sin. Therefore we can come boldly to the throne of grace that we may obtain mercy and find grace to help in time of need (Heb. 4:15–16). Thanks be to God for the greatest of all presents—Christ's matchless and glorious divine presence. Our Lord Jesus is able to keep us from falling, and to present us faultless before His glory with exceeding joy (Jude 1:24).

Every religion in the world prays. Rarely, however, do they hear the voice of the god to whom they pray.

Ignorance preserves and keeps dead religion afloat, without which it would be exposed and would sink quickly.

Religion does its own thing and then tries to slap God's name on it in an attempt to validate and gain credibility for its self-created counterfeit.

A tree is known by the fruit it produces. If your religion is not producing results in your life, leave it and never look back!

Stop seeking something and seek Someone, the Maker of heaven and Earth.

Truth is not a thing. Truth is a Person, and His name is Jesus.

Most ways lead astray, but when you follow Jesus, truth and life are freely yours today!

Chapter 7

Spirit and Truth

Truth is a forgotten aspect of spirituality in our day. People rarely ask questions anymore and blindly allow themselves to be led astray. Few are hungry enough to read the Bible and prayerfully study on their own to assess the validity of what they are hearing at the mosque, temple, or church.

I have always said that every religion in the world prays—rarely, however, do the followers of these religions hear the voice of the god to whom they pray. Most people outside of a religious setting are intelligent. Some people, once they enter a religious setting, suddenly discard their brain and reject all sound wisdom.

For example, if I were making a telephone call from Sri Lanka to America to speak to my mom, I would expect an international connection before agreeing to pay the telephone company for its services. If I could not first get through to the telephone operator to facilitate the connection, I would hang up the line and refuse to pay for such poor service.

Sadly, religious people are rarely as discerning with the truth. Many swallow lies in the name of religion and refuse to evaluate truth. Not expecting results in their lives, they allow their religion to pacify them, and lull them to sleep.

Spirit and Truth

Jesus boldly recognized such passivity in the woman at the well. He did not hesitate to tell her, "You [Samaritans] worship what you do not know" (John 4:22). The apostle Paul told the men of Athens, "Therefore, the One whom you worship without knowing, Him I proclaim to you" (Acts 17:23).

Ignorance preserves and keeps religion afloat, without which, it would be exposed and would quickly sink. God is looking for modern-day prophets like Jeremiah to "cry aloud, spare not" (Isa. 58:1). The earth is in need of many more John the Baptists to expose wickedness and lay the ax to the root of dead trees incapable of producing fruit (Luke 3:9). Every religion not birthed and planted in the earth by God will be uprooted and done away with (Matt. 15:13). The God of heaven will not allow Himself to be misrepresented by religion, nor will He tolerate the misuse of His holy name (Exod. 20:7).

Origins of Religion

Religion does its own thing and tries to slap God's name on it in an attempt to validate or gain credibility for its self-created counterfeit. Seeking to establish their own market niche in the religious world, many are quick to deify their movement and label anything but theirs a work of the devil. This exclusive attitude does not embody the heart of God the Father, who continually welcomes all of His children to follow Him and grow in grace as they move onward in their spiritual journey.

God vs. Religion

Religion has its origins both in man and demons. Doctrines are sets of beliefs and commandments adhered to by men. God's doctrine is powerful, unlike religious doctrines (Heb. 6:1–2; Luke 4:32). Religious doctrines, which do not originate from the heart of God, come from self-willed men and devilish spirits that inspire them (Matt. 15:3, 9; Mark 7:13; 1 Tim. 4:1).

Man-breathed and demon-inspired doctrines do not illuminate the souls of humanity. Entire nations and regions of the earth have been ensnared for centuries by unbiblical doctrines. In this hour, the Word of God must be known in spirit and truth, rightly divided, and properly discerned in every circumstance (2 Tim. 2:15). Seekers of God must become increasingly knowledgeable of Scripture to avoid being deceived by counterfeits. Many of them lie in wait to deceive unsuspecting and newborn babes in Christ (Eph. 4:14).

A tree is known by the fruit it produces. Therefore, we must become results oriented and stop accepting every doctrine or revelation that passes by just because it is the latest fad in the religious world. It is time we begin to know and follow God ourselves. It is time we get real and experience results.

Truth is not a thing. Truth is a Person, and His name is Jesus. The Lord unashamedly said, "I am the way, the truth, and the life" (John 14:6). Most ways lead astray, but when you follow Jesus, truth and life are freely yours. He produces results in the lives of His followers and assures them that they will hear His voice, because He is a living God (John 10:27). This is

Spirit and Truth

not so with other gods that are merely the creations of men and demons. They have no ability to speak as they are made with men's hands (Ps. 115:4–8). Yet, humans looking for something beyond themselves to talk to often engage and interact with such dead artifacts of religion. Even worse, they give their hard-earned money to them and get nothing in return. Paul preached throughout Asia, "They are not gods which are made with hands" (Acts 19:26).

What we tolerate will dominate. God will punish or reward us for our ways (Hos. 4:9). We must be discerning and fervent in spirit to rightly govern our spiritual lives. Otherwise, we will find ourselves under a spiritual pharaoh or praying to gods made with hands in bondage like everyone else.

The God of heaven has far better for us. Jesus said the Father delights for His children to worship Him in spirit and truth (John 4:24). Since the Holy Spirit is "the Spirit of truth" (John 16:13), it is impossible to have an expression of God's Spirit apart from truth.

Denominations often get a particular revelation or truth and build their churches on it. Then, they put a fence around their begotten truth and forget to press on into the full counsel of God. The fullness of the blessing of Christ does not take us into partial truth, but "all truth," allowing the Holy Spirit to lead and guide the way (Rom. 15:19, 29; John 16:13).

The Spirit of God knows and is releasing "present truth" to whoever has ears to hear today (2 Pet. 1:12; Mark 4:24). To merely cleave to denominational teachings is to thwart the work of the Spirit of God in your life, minimizing your effectiveness as a believer, and hindering the fullness of the blessing of Christ in and through you.

Sincerity alone does not determine whether or not a person will develop a meaningful relationship with God and not be bound by religion.

All you need to get to God is the faith of a child.

Jesus never gave His allegiance to any religion, church, or denomination.

No church can save you because no church died for you.

Keep your eyes on Jesus, the Author and Finisher of your faith.

Denominations are founded by men who err and eventually die.

No minister, ministry, church, or denomination can do for you what Jesus already has done for you.

The Holy Spirit is the means by which you access God on Earth.

Religion is full of ridicule and self-righteousness. Self-righteousness leads to self-exaltation, which is closely followed by the condemnation of others.

Religious people, who seemingly should be closest to Jesus and leading others to Him, are often the first to keep sincere people from Jesus.

The religious who are quick to condemn have more knowledge of God than relationship with God.

Religious people embrace the ministry of condemnation, but those who know Christ and the heart of God minister liberation and reconciliation.

Faith in Christ, not in your church, will set your heart and soul free.

Chapter 8

Religious Affiliation, Self-Exaltation, and Condemnation

One thing I dislike about religion is its divisive classifications. I love all of the peoples of the world, including those in the religious world, yet, I do not like how religions enslave us and denominations divide us. Positively speaking, I believe the people of God within the Christian denominations are sincere and truly hungry for God. Sincerity alone, however, does not determine whether a person will develop a meaningful relationship with God and not be bound by religion. Sadly, many sincere souls hoping to draw near to God are brought into bondage by religion. Many people embrace the traditions and ways of religion, because they think they are necessary to draw near to God. The only thing a person needs to get to God is the faith of a child.

Jesus did not join religious affiliations. He never gave His allegiance to any religion, church, or denomination, nor did He patronize them. No church can save you by itself because no church died for your sins. Jesus is not a Catholic or a Protestant. He was a loving Person who happily interacted with common people, who the religious elite rejected and despised.

Jesus does not have a political preference, nor is He a

member of a political party. When they came to make Jesus a King, he withdrew from them (John 6:15). Everyone who names the name of Christ throughout the denominations must follow Jesus. Christ is the Head of the church, not merely a man in religious attire. Jesus said, "I will build My church," against which the gates of hell will not prevail (Matt. 16:18). Jesus is building a spiritual house and the kingdom of God; neither of which give allegiance to any particular denomination (1 Pet. 2:5).

Do Not Hide Behind Religious Affiliations

The apostle Paul boldly addressed those who hid behind the religious denominations of their day, saying:

> For ye are yet carnal: for whereas there is among you envying, and strife, and divisions, are ye not carnal, and walk as men? For while one saith, I am of Paul; and another, I am of Apollos; are ye not carnal? Who then is Paul, and who is Apollos, but ministers by whom ye believed, even as the Lord gave to every man?
> —1 Corinthians 3:3–5, kjv

We are exhorted throughout Scripture to keep our eyes on Jesus. Denominations are founded by men who err and eventually die. Martin Luther led the Protestant reformation, which brought Christendom out of the Dark Ages. Yet he was anti-Semitic and continued to practice infant baptism—neither of which have any foundation in Scripture.

In this era we can be thankful for our forefathers in

the faith who blazed a trail unto freedom. Nevertheless we must pursue God to enter the fullness of the blessing of Christ and the totality of the counsel of God's Word. That means we must eat the fish and spit out the bones pertaining to the moves of God that preceded us.

Denominations are established upon truth as it was seen centuries ago. God wants you to be established in the very "present truth" (2 Pet. 1:12). Jesus sent the Holy Spirit to teach, lead, and guide us into "all truth" (John 16:12–13). No church should exalt itself to the place of the Godhead and Holy Trinity. No minister, ministry, church, or denomination can do for you what Jesus has already done for you. The Holy Spirit, through Christ, is the means by which you access God on Earth (Eph. 2:18).

Religion is exclusive and excessive. Jesus makes you acceptable to the Father in heaven and the Holy Spirit makes God accessible on Earth. Religion is full of ridicule and self-righteousness. Religious people often feel and project self-righteousness because of their successful adherence to rules and regulations. Self-righteousness can lead to self-exaltation, which is closely followed by the condemnation of others. Religious people often project a superior, "holier than thou" attitude without even knowing it. They might be heard saying, "'Keep to yourself, do not come near me, for I am holier than you!' These are smoke in My [God's] nostrils, a fire that burns all the day" (Isa. 65:5).

God dislikes pious attitudes that cause religious people to strut and parade around like peacocks, while

God vs. Religion

projecting their self-righteousness and ridiculing others in pursuit of God, who are not like them. Jesus told a parable concerning two men who went to pray:

> He spoke this parable to some who trusted in themselves that they were righteous, and despised others: "Two men went up to the temple to pray, one a Pharisee and the other a tax collector. The Pharisee stood and prayed thus with himself, 'God, I thank You that I am not like other men—extortioners, unjust, adulterers, or even as this tax collector. I fast twice a week; I give tithes of all that I possess.' And the tax collector, standing afar off, would not so much as raise his eyes to heaven, but beat his breast, saying, 'God, be merciful to me a sinner!' I tell you, this man went down to his house justified rather than the other; for everyone who exalts himself will be humbled, and he who humbles himself will be exalted."
>
> —Luke 18:9–14

One man during prayer boasted profusely about how great he was, and the other fell on his face before God pleading for mercy. Here is the vast difference between self-righteous, religious people, and those who want God despite their inadequacies. Religious people, who seemingly should be closest to Jesus and leading others to Him, are often the first to keep sincere people from Jesus:

> Then they also brought infants to Him that He might touch them; but when the disciples saw

Religious Affiliation, Self-Exaltation, and...

> it, they rebuked them. But Jesus called them to Him and said, "Let the little children come to Me, and do not forbid them; for of such is the kingdom of God. Assuredly, I say to you, whoever does not receive the kingdom of God as a little child will by no means enter it."
>
> —Luke 18:15–17

Notice how religious people operate. The disciples, who walked and talked with Jesus every day, were clueless concerning His heart toward people. The disciples thought kids were not important and wanted to shoo them away. Jesus, however, wanted the children to come to Him and feel welcomed. Religion justifies itself and condemns the innocent. Those who simply want to do the right thing and draw near to God, the Creator of heaven and Earth, are often condemned en route to Jesus. Such religious condemnation and despising of the lowly is an abomination to God:

> He who justifies the wicked, and he who condemns the just, both of them alike are an abomination to the Lord.
>
> —Proverbs 17:15

God knows very well who condemns. It is religious people who have just enough knowledge of God to be dangerous. The religious who are quick to condemn have more knowledge of God than relationship with God. Therefore they neither know nor show the heart of God to humanity:

> Who is he who condemns? It is Christ who died, and furthermore is also risen, who is even at the right hand of God, who also makes intercession for us.
> —Romans 8:34

Religious people embrace the ministering of condemnation, but those who know Christ and the heart of God minister healing and reconciliation. Condemnation leaves you feeling insecure and inadequate. The unconditional love and acceptance of God reconciles you to God the Father:

> There is therefore now no condemnation to those who are in Christ Jesus, who do not walk according to the flesh, but according to the Spirit.
> —Romans 8:1

Once you discover the glorious liberty in Christ that has been purchased for you on the cross at Calvary, you will not have to hide anymore behind your denominational affiliation. After all, Jesus is the Head of the church (Eph. 5:23). Faith in Christ, not in your church, will set your heart and soul free.

Pharisees want to give you hell and a piece of their mind. Jesus wants to give you heaven and a piece of His heart.

Religion hurts people by its ignorance and insensitivity. God, however, is gracious and kind, loving people wholeheartedly.

Your convictions, as good as they may be for you, should never be forced or pushed on somebody else. We should encourage obedience and adherence to the Bible, not our religious traditions and convictions.

How you interpret Scripture should never become a basis for another person's obedience. Each individual should be at liberty to discover, walk with, and enjoy God without coercion or intrusion.

God wants humanity to rest in Him, not in their religious works. God created the Sabbath for man as a day of rest, but religion only wants to question, debate, and test.

The only thing anyone must do is believe in Christ and what He has already done.

God is so simple it takes a theologian to complicate Him.

Chapter 9

Rigid and Frigid Rules

Religious people can become mean because they are unhappy or are unfulfilled in their lives. Because religion tries to represent God, people are quick to conform to its ways, thinking they will please God. The irony is that religion knows nothing about the heart and ways of God.

Before I came to Christ, I was a fun-loving, happy individual. I was even voted the funniest in my high school class. I was athletic and did well in school. But upon encountering God and experiencing a supernatural touch of the Holy Spirit, I went full force after heaven. Somewhere along the way, however, I became increasingly religious. I got rid of all my old friends and stopped associating with them, thinking that they might contaminate me and cause me to sin. I trusted God to bring me new friends, which He graciously did. However, when those new Christian friends arrived, I did not know how to properly relate to them.

Your Perception and Reality About God

Since I was not sure what was fitting and proper pertaining to Christian fun and interaction, I erred on the side of being extra cautious and doing "everything by the book." I did not tell jokes or clown around a whole

Rigid and Frigid Rules

lot. My interaction with my Christian friends consisted primarily of church, outreach, and prayer.

One evening my friends were going to play pool and asked me if I wanted to come along. I said no and gave some religious excuse, saying that I wanted to go pray. It was then that a friend confronted me and said, "You're being religious. It's OK to have fun, you know." It kind of shook me and challenged my religious mentality—and it was precisely what I needed. I stopped being legalistic and started learning how to have fun again. My fun-loving nature returned, and I began being myself again and learned how to relate to God properly. I resumed working as a lifeguard at a local water park, and started enjoying life again.

If you do not relate to God and see Him as He is, you might influence others with your warped concept of God. That is what the Pharisees did when they made converts. After they were done with them, they would be more bound than before they *got religion*. (Matt. 23:15).

Religionists often use condemnation, judgment, and the threat of the wrath of God to scare people into complying with their rigid rules. God's wrath, however, is revealed against religious fanatics, who suppress the truth by their wickedness (Rom. 1:18). God is all about love and grace. Religious people are quick to judge and get up in your face.

Religious people who project their righteousness onto others, while perverting the truth in order to serve their own interests, hinder sincere people from being able to reach our loving God. Such religious

God vs. Religion

people prefer their own self-righteousness, rather than submitting to God's righteousness.

> For they being ignorant of God's righteousness, and seeking to establish their own righteousness, have not submitted to the righteousness of God.
> —Romans 10:3

Jesus spoke to the multitudes and to His disciples, saying:

> The scribes and the Pharisees sit in Moses' seat. Therefore whatever they tell you to observe, that observe and do, but do not do according to their works; for they say, and do not do. For they bind heavy burdens, hard to bear, and lay them on men's shoulders; but they themselves will not move them with one of their fingers. But all their works they do to be seen by men. They make their phylacteries broad and enlarge the borders of their garments. They love the best places at feasts, the best seats in the synagogues, greetings in the marketplaces, and to be called by men, 'Rabbi, Rabbi.'
> —Matthew 23:2–7

Religion schools you in rules that nobody can live up to. No matter how much you do, it is never enough for religionists. That is because they live in a place of discontentment, and they will never be satisfied until they have your company in their misery.

God in heaven looks at the heart, but religion is enamored with the outward appearance and tells

Rigid and Frigid Rules

people how to dress and wear their hair. The religious leaders in Jesus' day complained about people not washing their hands, but they themselves had unclean hearts (Luke 11:37–39). Religious oppressors are ravenous wolves in sheep's clothing (Matt. 10:16). They talk the talk, but refuse to walk the walk.

****

Nothing you can do will ever be enough to satisfy the insatiable appetite of religion. Religion will not rest until it wears you out, devours you, and takes you deep into the wilderness to abandon you. What Christ did on the cross at Calvary is sufficient for humanity. Religion, however, will never have tranquility, because it is focused not on Christ, but on self and its inadequacy. Jesus knew this about religion and could see through the religious leaders. He boldly rebuked them, saying, "Blind guides, who strain out a gnat and swallow a camel" (Matt. 23:24).

Ignorant, Ugly, and Insensitive

Religion is ugly and insensitive. The Creator is beautiful and attractive. Life is challenging enough as it is. We do not need anything, such as religion, to complicate our lives any further. Religion pushes; Jesus gently leads and allows you to follow. Following is a perfect example of the heart of religion and how burdensome it can be to sincere people:

> And he said to them, "What advice do you give? How should we answer this people who have spoken to me, saying, 'Lighten the yoke which your father put on us'?" Then the young men who had grown up with him spoke to him, saying, "Thus you should speak to this people who have spoken to you, saying, 'Your father made our yoke heavy, but you make it lighter on us'—thus you shall say to them: 'My little finger shall be thicker than my father's waist! And now, whereas my father put a heavy yoke on you, I will add to your yoke; my father chastised you with whips, but I will chastise you with scourges!'"
>
> —1 KINGS 12:9–11

Unlike religion, Jesus is not interested in putting yokes on people. Jesus is in the business of removing yokes from people. Religionists rigidly adhere to the letter of the law and are quick to condemn. Jesus is loving, gracious, and ready to mend. Fundamentalism is intolerant, self-righteous, and sour in its presentation of God. God, however, does not need to work on and fuss over His presentation because His presence is sufficient. There is no fun in fundamentalism, but there is much fun in God. The Taliban in Afghanistan wants to keep people under its heavy hand. God the Father, through Christ, wants to set us free and liberate the land.

Pharisees want to give you hell and a piece of their mind. Jesus wants to give you heaven and a piece of His heart. Jesus is intolerant of sin, but very welcoming and tolerant of people. Jesus said:

Rigid and Frigid Rules

Take My yoke upon you and learn from Me, for I am gentle and lowly in heart, and you will find rest for your souls. For My yoke is easy and My burden is light.

—Matthew 11:29–30

Then the scribes and Pharisees brought to Him a woman caught in adultery. And when they had set her in the midst, they said to Him, "Teacher, this woman was caught in adultery, in the very act. Now Moses, in the law, commanded us that such should be stoned. But what do You say?" This they said, testing Him, that they might have something of which to accuse Him. But Jesus stooped down and wrote on the ground with His finger, as though He did not hear. So when they continued asking Him, He raised Himself up and said to them, "He who is without sin among you, let him throw a stone at her first." And again He stooped down and wrote on the ground. Then those who heard it, being convicted by their conscience, went out one by one, beginning with the oldest even to the last. And Jesus was left alone, and the woman standing in the midst. When Jesus had raised Himself up and saw no one but the woman, He said to her, "Woman, where are those accusers of yours? Has no one condemned you?" She said, "No one, Lord." And Jesus said to her, "Neither do I condemn you; go and sin no more."

—John 8:3–11

God vs. Religion

> Then I heard a loud voice saying in heaven, "Now salvation, and strength, and the kingdom of our God, and the power of His Christ have come, for the accuser of our brethren, who accused them before our God day and night, has been cast down."
> —Revelation 12:10

> The anointing of the Holy Spirit destroys yokes of bondage from our lives.
> —Isaiah 10:27

Religion hurts people with its ignorance and insensitivity. God, however, is gracious and kind, loving people wholeheartedly. Because of God's great love, He sent the Holy Spirit to help us in our weaknesses (Rom. 8:26).

Even after Jesus rose from the dead and ascended into heaven, religious leaders continually sought to bring the apostles under bondage by their rigid rules and regulations. One group of religious legalists said, "Unless you are circumcised according to the custom of Moses, you cannot be saved" (Acts 15:1).

The apostles, after much discussion and prayer, decided not to give place to such religious legalism. They were fully persuaded that salvation is by grace through faith, not of works. Today, in Christ, we need to cut away ungodliness and worldliness (Rom. 2:28–29; Jer. 4:4). The apostles boldly stood up to the Judaic leaders and said:

> So God, who knows the heart, acknowledged them by giving them the Holy Spirit, just as He did to us, and made no distinction between us

Rigid and Frigid Rules

and them, purifying their hearts by faith. Now therefore, why do you test God by putting a yoke on the neck of the disciples which neither our fathers nor we were able to bear? But we believe that through the grace of the Lord Jesus Christ we shall be saved in the same manner as they.
—Acts 15:8–11

****

Freedom is not free! To forever secure our freedoms, we must fight to maintain freedom's values and beliefs. We must guard against ideologies that would usurp and war against our freedoms:

> Stand fast therefore in the liberty by which Christ has made us free, and do not be entangled again with a yoke of bondage.
> —Galatians 5:1

> Then you shall call, and the Lord will answer; you shall cry, and He will say, "Here I am." If you take away the yoke from your midst, the pointing of the finger, and speaking wickedness…Then your light shall dawn in the darkness.
> —Isaiah 58:9–10

Taking away the yoke means not troubling or burdening people with yokes of bondage. Such yokes often come in the form of religious rules, beliefs, or convictions. Your convictions, as good as they may be for you, should never be forced or pushed on somebody else. We should encourage obedience and adherence to the Bible, not our religious traditions and convictions. How you interpret Scripture should never become a basis for another person's obedience. Each individual should be at liberty to discover, walk with, and enjoy God without coercion or intrusion.

Religion violates people. God gives people willpower. Religion strips people of personal power. God empowers people to make their own decisions. God wants humanity to rest in Him, not in their religious works. God created the Sabbath for man as a day of rest, but religion only wants to question, debate, and test. "There remains therefore a rest for the people of God" (Heb. 4:9). Religion never rests. Religion's conscience and eternal security revolve around what one does, not what Jesus has done. Therefore, religious people are continually restless.

God's children trust Him. The deception of religion is that you must do things. The only thing anyone must do is believe in Christ and what He has already done. Jesus is the wonderful Prince of Peace (Isa. 9:6–7). Peace eludes the religious and finds the simple believer in Christ. God is so simple it takes a theologian to complicate Him. Live simply and simply live. Look unto Jesus, the Author and Finisher of your faith. Peace like a river is found in Christ alone. On Christ the solid Rock I stand—religion is but sinking sand.

Ironically, religion knows little about the heart and ways of God.

Dumb doctrines and convictions make unhappy people.

Religion always makes you big in your own eyes and in the religious community. God, however, causes you to realize His greatness, after which you walk humbly with Jesus and happily remain small in your own eyes.

God progressively reveals and makes Himself known to mankind.

The extent that we know God as He is determines the extent to which we experience God as He is.

Most people stop at their first revelation of Jesus.

Religion tries to change you from the outside in, making you conform and line up to all its rules and regulations. Divine change occurs from the inside out.

God Almighty is not in a hurry. God is love, which is patient and kind. Religion is a hard taskmaster that is never satisfied.

The devil is the father of lies and accuser of the brethren. Therein is his whole strategy against humanity.

Being a religious recluse that lives within a cave is not Christlike. Jesus came to seek and save the lost, not to hide and hold out until the end of the age.

The kingdom of God is not meat and drink, but righteousness, peace, and joy in the Holy Spirit.

Whether you eat or drink, or whatever you do, do all to the glory of God.

Religion is void of spiritual discernment as it looks at the outward rather than the inward. God looks at the heart within.

The Holy Spirit is the insoluble force to the Godhead. The Holy Spirit is the means on Earth by which we access the Father and the Son in heaven.

There is no competition in the Holy Trinity. The Holy Spirit glorifies Jesus and Christ glorifies the Father.

God resists the proud.

Islam is a fatherless religion that historically has been spread by the sword.

If any angel or spirit deviates and departs from the Word of God, reject it wholeheartedly.

Chapter 10

Dumb Doctrines and Convictions

Your perception of God determines your personal reality of Him. To Abraham, God was a God of blessing—Abraham was blessed. To Moses, God was a Deliverer—Moses became a deliverer. To Elijah, God was a God of justice and fire—Elijah called fire down from heaven. To David, God was a King—David became king. To the Pharisees, God was a God of guilt and judgment—the Pharisees were quick to pass judgment and make others feel guilty. Dumb doctrines and erroneous personal convictions make for unhappy people. (See Genesis 12:2–3; Exodus 3:7–8; 1 Kings 18:21–24; 1 Samuel 16:1–13; Matthew 23:23.)

Jesus said, "According to your faith let it be to you" (Matt. 9:29). This is why Jesus sought to know what other people, including His disciples, thought about Him. The Lord asked Peter directly, "Who do you say that I am?" (Matt. 16:15). Jesus boldly told the woman at the well, "You worship what you do not know" (John 4:22). Her perception about God was off, as she thought worship had to take place in some geographical place to get God's blessing (v. 20). This is no different than the Muslims in our day who feel they must pray facing Mecca.

Saul was a radical Jew who went about killing

God vs. Religion

Christians until Jesus supernaturally visited his life. Jesus appeared in His glory to Saul, after which he was blind for three days (Acts 9:1–9; 26:12–14). When Jesus appeared to him, Saul sobered up real quick and humbly cried out, "Who are You, Lord?" (Acts 26:15).

It was evident by the brightness of the glory that had visited Saul that whoever it was, He alone was God. Immediately Saul was changed from a murderer of Christians to a messenger for the resurrected Christ! That is the kind of transformation that can occur in the twinkling of an eye when you see God as He is.

Most merely see God as they think Him to be. That is why the Vatican paid Michelangelo to paint a blonde-haired, blue-eyed Jesus. The Pope and Europeans wanted God to look European; however, Jesus was from Israel and probably had the darker features of a man from the Middle East.

Some African Christians contend that Jesus was black. Over in Asia, some Chinese believe Jesus was Chinese. All of them are missing the boat when they identify with God as a mere man and do not know Him by His Spirit. Though Jesus came in the flesh, after the Resurrection we are to know Him not by the flesh but by the Spirit (2 Cor. 5:16).

God appeared to and delivered Saul from his religion and legalistic lifestyle so that he could go open the eyes of others, deliver them from darkness to light, and display the power of God to his generation (Acts 26:16–18; 1 Cor. 2:4–5). God changed Saul's nature and name, calling him Paul. The name *Paul* means "little" in the

Dumb Doctrines and Convictions

original Greek. It also means "strength in God."[1]

Religion leaves you weak within, but always makes you big in your own eyes and in the religious community. God, however, causes people to realize His greatness so they can walk humbly with Jesus and happily remain small in their own eyes. Then you can be strong in the Lord and the power of His might (Eph. 6:10).

Paul confronted the men of Athens, telling them how religious and ignorant they were:

> Then Paul stood in the midst of the Areopagus and said, "Men of Athens, I perceive that in all things you are very religious; for as I was passing through and considering the objects of your worship, I even found an altar with this inscription: TO THE UNKNOWN GOD. Therefore, the One whom you worship without knowing, Him I proclaim to you: God, who made the world and everything in it, since He is Lord of heaven and earth, does not dwell in temples made with hands. Nor is He worshiped with men's hands, as though He needed anything, since He gives to all life, breath, and all things."
>
> —Acts 17:22–25

God said to Moses, "I am the Lord. I appeared to Abraham, to Isaac, and to Jacob, as God Almighty, but by My name Lord I was not known to them" (Exod. 6:2–3). God reveals Himself to mankind to the extent that we seek Him as He is. This can determine the extent to which we experience God as He is. Some see Jesus as the Savior of their sins but do not submit to Him as

God vs. Religion

Lord. Others believe God can forgive their sins, but have no faith that He can also heal their diseases. Even fewer people believe God will prosper them financially.

We must pursue the Personhood of God to fully discover and experience Him. Most people stop at their first revelation of Jesus. They see Christ on the cross as the suffering Messiah, but never get to know Him as the conquering King who victoriously rose from the grave. Therefore they never experience God's power, nor do they live in victory. You cannot show in your own life what you do not first know in your own heart about God:

> For now we see in a mirror, dimly, but then face to face. Now I know in part, but then I shall know just as I am also known.
> —1 Corinthians 13:12

> Beloved, now we are children of God; and it has not yet been revealed what we shall be, but we know that when He is revealed, we shall be like Him, for we shall see Him as He is.
> —1 John 3:2

Presently we know God only in part, as we have never seen Him in His fullness nor face to face. Therefore we must walk humbly before God and continue to press in to know Him more. The great apostle Paul wrote two-thirds of the New Testament. Yet he humbly admitted that he had not arrived. Paul followed hard after God saying, "That I may know Him and the power of His resurrection, and the fellowship of His sufferings, being conformed to His death, if, by any means, I may attain to the resurrection from the dead. Not that I have already attained, or am already perfected; but I press on, that I may lay hold of that for which Christ Jesus has also laid hold of me (Phil. 3:10–12).

Be Happy and Holy

Sadly, there are many socially dysfunctional people in the church. I know because I used to be one. It is good for socially dysfunctional people to go to church. Newcomers, however, often bump into these dysfunctional types in church and get a distorted image of God. Newborn babes in Christ cross paths with these "seasoned saints" who have lost the joy of the Lord and come under legalism when they are told all of the things they have to do to measure up. Unfortunately, over time many believers in Christ become increasingly religious and lose the joy of their salvation. They lose their first love and passion for God. It can happen to all of us if we are not careful. Sometimes the deadest people in church can even be those leading the service on the platform.

If young believers are not careful, they can succumb to such religiosity and soon they too will be in bondage, but it will be a different kind of bondage, called religious legalism. Religious bondage is a far worse enslavement than sin.

It is a narrow path that enters into life. This is the highway of holiness that is full of happiness, not legalism. Many people have not learned the art of being both happy and holy. They usually emphasize one or the other. Typically people who only focus on the holiness of God are not too happy. They forget that He is a gracious and loving Father. Happy people who love God very often can live holy because they want to please their Father in heaven.

The Bible says the joy of the Lord is our strength (Neh. 8:10). Trying in your own strength to be holy will not strengthen you spiritually. Holiness is not something you strive for. Holiness is something that can only be achieved as you welcome the Holy Spirit to live in you and work the holiness of God in and through your life (Phil. 2:12–13).

Divine change occurs from the inside out. Religion tries to change you from the outside in, making you conform and line up to all its rules and regulations. Religion is rigid and frigid. God is more natural and free, allowing the process of sanctification to occur in you.

Since Lucifer was expelled from the presence of God, he has been doing his best to constantly misrepresent God. The devil is skilled at quoting Scripture out of context and condemning people.

The devil is the father of lies (John 8:44). The Bible calls Satan the "accuser of our brethren" (Rev. 12:10), and that is his whole strategy against humanity. Lying spirits are demonic messengers of Satan that come to accuse, condemn, and belittle you. They whisper in your ear, "God doesn't love you. You're not doing it right. You think you are so holy, but I know what you did last week. You filthy sinner! God won't accept you."

The only way to overcome Satan's lies is to know the

truth and boldly declare God's Word over your life. Jesus defeated Satan in His hour of temptation by repeatedly saying, "It is written" (Matt. 4; Luke 4). We too must use the same spiritual weapons, beginning with the sword of the Spirit, which is the Word of God (Eph. 6:10–18).

Another useful spiritual weapon at our disposal is the shield of faith. By this, we can extinguish all of the fiery darts (lies and accusations) of the enemy. Once you know who God is, based on His Word, and are confident concerning His heart toward you, you can rest secure in who you are in Christ. It does not matter what any demon says about you. Faith comes by hearing the Word of God (Rom. 10:17). As you dig in to know the Word and heart of God, His ways and His will shall be made known to you.

Convictions and Condemnation

Another religious stumbling block of many good-hearted people going after God is personal convictions. We all have personal convictions, yet we should never elevate our personal convictions to the place of holy writ and try to make others conform to them. The Bible is our living manual, not your convictions. So if you personally choose not to drink, do not try to make people feel they are evil for having a glass of wine. Jesus said, "Not what goes into the mouth defiles a man; but what comes out of the mouth" (Matt. 15:11). Being a religious, unloving Pharisee to people for having a beer is just as bad, if not worse, than the beer itself.

GOD VS. RELIGION

My deceased mother was an alcoholic and drug addict, so I am well aware of the dangers of substance abuse. Yet I am also aware of the dangers of disassociating with humanity (in an attempt to preserve personal purity) whom Christ would have us win to Him for eternity. Being a religious recluse that lives in a cave is not Christlike. Jesus came to "seek and to save that which was lost" (Luke 19:10), not to hide and hold out until the end of the age. He happily associated with all people and was known to be "a friend of…sinners" (Luke 7:34).

The apostle Paul himself became "all things to all men, that [he] might by all means save some" (1 Cor. 9:22). Paul ate baklava with the Greeks and whatever else was put before him when with people. He and Timothy were circumcised to fit in with the Jews who they sought to win to Christ (Acts 16:1–4; Phil. 3:5).

All People and Food Are Acceptable

God loves everybody no matter the color of their skin. Our God is a colorful Creator. Look at the variety of animals at the nearest zoo and see for yourself. Religion discriminates between different people and food. Satan—old slue foot[1]—saw in people's fleshly appearance a means by which to divide humanity. So he put it in our hearts to fight one another instead of love each other. The devil cleverly saw in the food we eat each day another way to divide us.

God likes variety and individuality. For this reason,

---

1 "Slue foot" is a term for the devil.

He created the different kinds of people and their endless variations of food throughout the earth. Our Creator takes joy in His people.

> For every creature of God is good, and nothing is to be refused if it is received with thanksgiving.
> —1 TIMOTHY 4:4

The apostle Peter was changed by God in order for him to stop being prejudiced against the Gentiles. Peter thought God only liked the Jews. God told Peter, "Kill and eat" (Acts 10:13). Thereafter Peter saw the Holy Spirit poured out on the Gentiles while he ministered to them. It was then that Peter realized God was not just talking about certain foods being acceptable but also all peoples (Acts 10). God is no respecter of persons, but in every nation, he that fears God and works righteousness is accepted by Him (Acts 10:34–35).

Enjoy, But Do Not Be Offensive

Jesus liked to eat. When the Pharisees commented on the fact that He and His disciples did not fast, Jesus basically said, "They can fast when I'm gone, but as long as I'm here, we're eating" (Matt. 9:14–15, author's paraphrase). Even after His resurrection, Jesus ate some fish (John 21). When Christ and His church are together in heaven, the first order of ceremony is the marriage supper of the Lamb (Rev. 19:9, 17). Once God's people got a hold of this revelation, they began to eat, drink, and be merry. They were gathering everyday for food, fun, and fellowship (Acts 2:41–47). The church grew exponentially by the thousands.

With all of that church growth, God had to raise and send men like Paul to clean His house. Where there is a lot of eating, things can get messy. The apostle Paul had to bring order to the churches because they were out of control. Paul did not tell them to stop. He simply asked them to be respectful when they were in God's house and to not be offensive to people who were weak or new in their faith. Paul had to rebuke them because they were coming to God's house and taking communion out of order. One was eating before the other instead of eating and drinking in unison. Others were apparently getting drunk on the cup intended to remember Christ's suffering. Paul said, "Do you not have houses to eat and drink in? Or do you despise the church of God?" (1 Cor. 11:22).

> The kingdom of God is not eating and drinking, but righteousness and peace and joy in the Holy Spirit.
>
> —ROMANS 14:17

Paul exhorted the believers to walk in love and not grieve others with what they ate. Paul thought it was better to forego a certain food or drink to maintain peace and unity with the brethren (Rom. 14:15). He said, "Do not destroy the work of God for the sake of food. All things indeed are pure, but it is evil for the man who eats with offense" (Rom. 14:20).

The desire to win souls drove the apostle Paul. He would dare to eat strange and unusual things when

Dumb Doctrines and Convictions

he was with unsaved people in order to connect with them and hopefully win them to Christ. Paul, therefore, encouraged believers to be respectful when eating with people of other cultures and customs:

> Eat whatever is sold in the meat market, asking no questions for conscience' sake; for "the earth is the Lord's, and all its fullness."
> —1 Corinthians 10:24–25

Paul dealt with all of the believers in the early church and their hang-ups pertaining to foods and the observance of holy days (1 Cor. 8:10; Rom. 14). God even gave the apostle Peter a supernatural visitation to assure and strengthen him in the truth pertaining to this (Acts 10).

> For there is no distinction between Jew and Greek, for the same Lord over all is rich to all who call upon Him.
> —Romans 10:12

So pertaining to your own dietary intake of food, if you have faith, eat happily whatever you like. If you are persuaded in your own conscience that you should not eat something, don't eat it. But don't make your personal convictions into religious law, by which you harass and enslave others. For those of you who know the truth and abide in faith, don't boast and ridicule those who choose to adhere to a stricter dietary standard. Consider your own health also and know that moderation and discretion is advantageous.

Do you have faith? Have it to yourself before

God vs. Religion

> God. Happy is he who does not condemn himself in what he approves.
> —ROMANS 14:22

> Whether you eat or drink, or whatever you do, do all to the glory of God.
> —1 CORINTHIANS 10:31

Dumb Doctrines

Dumb doctrines lead to bound up, unsatisfied people. Therefore we must take the Word of God and, like skillful surgeons, set the captives free. At the same time, we are called to continue interacting lovingly and patiently with those who oppose themselves by holding to limiting beliefs, false doctrines, and deadly assumptions. Pray that the Holy Spirit will enlighten them to the knowledge of the truth, illuminate their hearts, and lead them into His marvelous light.

Religious exclusion by color or culture

In the early days of their religion, Mormons said that black people were cursed. Such beliefs are demonic and not scriptural. God loves all the peoples of the world (John 3:16) and blesses whoever will come to Him through His Son Jesus (John 14:6). The best churches in the world are those where there are many ethnic groups coming together in unity (Ps. 133; Acts 13).

Religious legalism concerning certain meats

It is well known that excessive indulgence in anything is not healthy. Moderation should be practiced with the consumption of anything. Abstinence, however, is a matter of personal conviction, not doctrine. Yet the Seventh Day Adventists have seemingly made the Law of Moses their present-day creed, based on their strict adherence to dietary laws and observance of the Sabbath. The law given by God to Moses is good (Rom. 7:12). If you live by it, you will probably live longer and stronger. Nevertheless to legalistically preach that to be pleasing to God you must adhere to this dietary law is unscriptural according to the New Testament. All Old Testament truths must be pulled through the cross of Christ to ascertain their level of importance in the present age and dispensation of grace in which we live.

We should not allow our belly to become our god. Abstinence from certain meats does not commend us to God; for we are neither better nor worse if we eat something (1 Cor. 8:8). The apostles decided we should simply abstain from meats offered to idols, and from blood, and from things strangled (Acts 15:29). This was more so for spiritual and health reasons so as to not seemingly or unnecessarily exalt a foreign god and endanger oneself of becoming ill.

Religious regulations and outward appearances

When I ministered throughout Malawi, Africa, during the summer of 1994, I encountered religious doctrines and convictions that restricted certain clothing for women. The longstanding president of twenty-five years apparently passed some law in which women were not permitted to wear pants. They could only wear dresses.

God vs. Religion

The Bible does not forbid women to wear pants. Modesty is encouraged in Scripture, but the forbidding of a certain type of clothing is nowhere to be found. God allows us each to be guided from within by the Holy Spirit pertaining to what is appropriate. Of course throughout time, religious leaders have sought to mandate their convictions and preferences pertaining to clothing, but nowhere is this mandated in holy writ.

When the first presidential election in Malawi was finally held, the Christian president who had been in power for decades lost the election. His legalistic approach to modesty certainly did not help him get the vote of women. Sadly, many godly people with good intentions get twisted up in religious legalism after which they lose their influence in society.

People do not deserve to be controlled and told what to do in the name of religion. Jesus came to set the captives free, not to take them into captivity (Luke 4:18). The Holy Spirit is the spirit of liberty (2 Cor. 3:17).

God looks at the heart within, not at the length of your hair or style of your clothes (1 Sam. 16:7). Jesus said, "Do not judge according to appearance, but judge with righteous judgment" (John 7:24). Religiosity is void of spiritual discernment as it looks at the outward rather than celebrating the inward.

> Stand fast therefore in the liberty by which Christ has made us free, and do not be entangled again with a yoke of bondage.
> —GALATIANS 5:1

Dumb Doctrines and Convictions

Those who seek to create religious rules and legalistic codes for us to follow are false brethren, who desire to remove us from the liberty wherewith Christ has made us free. They only want to bring us into bondage (Gal. 2:4). Religious misery loves company. Do not give ear or place to them in your heart and mind for a moment. Such religious rules void of the foundation of Scripture are weak and unspiritual (Gal. 4:9).

When God made Adam and Eve, He put them in the garden naked and not ashamed. Man and woman were made in God's image. When Jesus returns and restores the earth to the Father, the glory of God will so radiate and reign that there will be no need for the sun, because there shall be no night anymore (Isa. 60:19–20; Rev. 21:23; 22:5). God's glory will brilliantly shine and illuminate mankind.

Jesus blasted the religious leaders for being overly focused on the outward appearance. Jesus said to his disciples, "Beware of the scribes, who desire to go around in long robes, love greetings in the marketplaces, the best seats in the synagogues, and the best places at feasts, who devour widows' houses, and for a pretense make long prayers. These will receive greater condemnation" (Luke 20:45–47). The guys in the long robes of religion will be the first to receive greater damnation according to Jesus.

No-music doctrine

Some religious groups choose not to use music. That is perfectly fine. Yet when they take their personal preference and legalistically make a religious rule out of it, saying God does not permit music in church, that is *not* OK. God is musical and loves music (Ps. 149:3; 150). When the Creator formed the three archangels, He made Lucifer to preside over music. Lucifer had an orchestra in himself by which to lead praise and worship (Ezek. 28:13).

God tells us in His Word to enter His presence with singing (Ps. 100:2). David, the man after God's own heart, danced triumphantly when the ark of God was brought forth with music and jubilee (2 Sam. 6:14–15). Samuel and the company of the prophets were very musical (1 Sam. 10:5). The prophet Elisha recognized that a musical minstrel could bless God and stir the anointing of His presence to prophesy (2 Kings 3:15–16). David discovered that when he played the harp, demon power was broken in the presence of the Lord (1 Sam. 16:23).

Churches that go without music do not know what they are missing. Not to mention they will not have many young people in attendance. Elvis had a great musical gift that his church rejected so he took it into the world to be celebrated. Had Elvis been embraced by the church, he might still be alive today.

Let everything that has breath praise the Lord! (Ps. 150:6).

Jehovah's Witnesses ("JWs")

Jehovah's Witnesses, as they call themselves, claim Jesus is not God. I beg to differ as God the Father calls His Son God and tells all the angels to worship Him

(Heb. 1:5–6, 8). Other Scripture passages that affirm the deity of Christ are found throughout the Bible: Matthew 2:11, John 1:1–14, John 8:58, John 11:25, and John 3:16. The JW's *New World Translation* has rewritten all of these passages to remove any divine references to Jesus.

I have been to some kingdom halls where the JWs worship and have seen their children. I did not think that they looked very happy. They are not allowed to celebrate their birthdays, Christmas, or any other holiday. If they were ever in a medical emergency, JWs are against their people receiving blood transfusions. These precious people need an infusion of the Spirit of truth to set them free from deception and error.

Opposition to the Trinity

Many religious sects and even a few Christians oppose the doctrine of the Trinity. Some say we are to baptize in Jesus' name only. In the beginning, however, God the Father said, "Let Us make man in Our image" (Gen. 1:26). When the eternal purposes of God needed to be established in the earth, a voice came from heaven saying, "Who will go for Us?" (Isa. 6:8). Both of these uses of the pronoun *us* are references to a plural entity, in this case the holy Trinity.

Jesus consistently recognized God the Father and God the Holy Spirit. Jesus said, "I can of Myself do nothing" (John 5:19, 30). JWs distort and misinterpret these passages to deny the deity of Christ when proselytizing from house to house. What they fail to realize is that Jesus relied upon the power of the Holy

God vs. Religion

Spirit with whom He had an intimate relationship (2 Cor. 13:14; Phil. 2:1). This is why Jesus said there is no forgiveness for those who blaspheme the Holy Spirit (Luke 12:10). The Holy Spirit is the insoluble force to the Godhead (Mic. 3:8; Luke 5:17; Phil. 1:19).

It is "'not by might nor by power, but by My Spirit,' says the LORD" (Zech. 4:6). The apostle Peter recognized the Holy Spirit as God (Acts 5:3–4). Jesus and God the Father are in heaven. It was the Holy Spirit who raised Christ from the dead (Rom. 8:11). The Holy Spirit is the means on Earth by which we access the Father and the Son in heaven (Eph. 2:18). Jesus taught His disciples to pray to the Father in His name (Matt. 6:9; John 14:14).

Jesus told Philip, "He who has seen Me has seen the Father... The words that I speak to you I do not speak on My own authority; but the Father who dwells in Me does the works. Believe Me that I am in the Father and the Father in Me, or else believe Me for the sake of the works themselves" (John 14:7–11).

Being *in* the Father is accomplished through the Holy Spirit. Jesus told the disciples the Holy Spirit would be "in" and "with" them (John 14:16–17). We who are in Christ are "one spirit" (1 Cor. 6:17), even as the Son and Father in heaven are one (Mark 16:19).

There is no competition in the Holy Trinity. The Holy Spirit glorifies Jesus (John 16:13–14) and Christ glorifies the Father (John 12:28). These three are "One," expressed in three Persons (Deut. 6:4). This is a truth and mystery that is spiritually discerned. Such truths appear foolish to the carnal minded (1 Cor. 2:14). Without the Holy

Dumb Doctrines and Convictions

Spirit, human beings are incapable of obeying divine commandments. It is the Holy Spirit who melts us within and gives us a heart to obey (Ezek. 36:26–27).

Roman Catholics

The Vatican makes a great show of religion. I admit they have some of the most beautiful buildings, Christian paintings, and artifacts around the world, however, some of their religious practices do not exalt God the Father nor Jesus the Son.

Praying to Mary is nowhere to be found in Scripture. Prayer to the queen of heaven is a pagan concept that brings great anger to God (Jer. 7:18; Acts 19:27). Mary the mother of Jesus recognized her need for a Savior (Luke 1:47). Mary said concerning Jesus, "Whatever He says to do, do it" (John 2:5). Jesus never deified Mary, nor did any of His disciples. To do so today is both erroneous and deceptive, therefore, do not pray to Mary. Pray to God the Father in Jesus' name.

Some people out of respect want to see the pope. They will travel across the world to meet him, which is perfectly fine. What is not permissible is exalting the pope to the place of God. We should not bow down and worship a man. Jesus is the only pope according to holy writ (1 Tim. 6:15).

Roman Catholics claim Peter was the first pope. When Cornelius came to see Peter, he bowed down before him. For what reason Cornelius bowed to Peter, we do not know. Whether it was out of respect, holy fear, reverence, or worship is unclear. What we do know is

Peter did not permit or tolerate anybody to bow before him. Peter told Cornelius, "Stand up; I myself am also a man" (Acts 10:24–26).

Let us remember that the true prophet points you to Jesus and does not want the glory for himself (John 3:30), but this is not so with religion that seeks to build its own kingdom and exalt itself.

Celibacy is enforced upon the priesthood by the Vatican, though it is not scriptural. Forbidding the priesthood to marry was called a doctrine of demons by the apostle Paul (1 Timothy 4:1–3). Many priests have had to suppress their God-given sexual desires in order to remain in the priesthood. Sadly, some of those repressed desires have resulted in a few priests practicing pedophelia. Truly, it is better to marry than to burn (1 Cor. 7:9).

I want the best for my Catholic brethren. The fullness of the blessing of Christ is available to whosoever will seek the Lord. Enter the light and truth of God's Word, and exercise humility. God resists the proud. We can have more if we do not settle for less.

Muslims

Moderate Muslims have been given a bad name by the jihadist killers within Islam. Most people, whatever their religion, desire to live peacefully with others. What we must realize about the Islamic militants is that they are following the Quran, their holy book which encourages the killing of infidels.

God the Father (as the Bible teaches) is not a killer, but a Lifegiver. Jesus said that in the last days people

Dumb Doctrines and Convictions

would come in the name of God killing others, thinking that they are serving God (John 16:1–3). They do this because they do not know God.

Allah is a pagan moon god and not the God of the Bible. There are no references in the Quran to Allah being a loving father who rejoices over his children. Allah is a mean, angry god. Islam is a fatherless religion that has been historically spread by the sword, hence the presence of the sword in many Islamic nations' flags.

Mohammad did not get his revelation from God but rather from an angel. Mohammad claimed that the angel Gabriel visited him. The prophets throughout the Bible heard from God directly and did not go through angels (Isaiah to Malachi). They heard the voice of God and were shown visions from the Lord. The apostle Paul exhorted, "If we, or an angel from heaven, preach any other gospel to you than what we have preached to you, let him be accursed" (Gal. 1:8).

Mohammad questioned his revelation concerning his prophetic ministry, thinking he was demon possessed. Mohammad was epileptic and often had seizures, something that was considered demonic in his day. This is certainly not what I look for in a prophet and founder of a religion. Uncertainty is deadly. Whatever is not of faith is sin (Rom. 14:23).

God teaches us to always try the spirits that influence us and make sure that they line up with Scripture. The Father, the Word, and the Holy Spirit always agree (1 John 5:7). If any angel or spirit deviates and departs from the Word of God, reject it wholeheartedly.

Mormonism

Mormons historically have practiced polygamy. Like Muslim men, some Mormons still do. Mormons believe that in heaven they will populate numerous planets by procreation, thus they have a fleshly concept of heaven.

Jesus said there will be no marrying in heaven as we will then have glorified bodies like the angels (Luke 20:34–36). Jesus preached a spiritual heaven and established His spiritual kingdom within the hidden heart of man.

Like Mohammad, Joseph Smith, the founder of Mormonism, also claimed to have been visited by angels. Smith also left the authority of holy Scripture, seeking to add his revelation to the knowledge of God's Word. He and Mohammed are false prophets—if the root is false, so also are the foundation and religious structure.

The book of Mormon is a perversion and addition to the Word of God. Mormonism preaches another Jesus other than the Jesus of the Bible (2 Cor. 11:2–4). Mormonism teaches that Jesus came to America and started their movement. Nothing is farther from the truth! America is not special above other nations in the eyes of God. God so loves the world that Jesus said when He returns to Earth every eye shall see Him (Matt. 24:26–27; Rev. 1:7).

> Let no one cheat you of your reward, taking delight in false humility and worship of angels, intruding into those things which he has not seen, vainly puffed up by his fleshly mind.
> —COLOSSIANS 2:18

Dumb Doctrines and Convictions

> For I testify to everyone who hears the words of the prophecy of this book: If anyone adds to these things, God will add to him the plagues that are written in this book.
> —Revelation 22:18

Hindus

I have been to India five times and lived there for nine months. I have never met an Indian who has visited more of their country than I have. During my travels throughout the country, I noticed that the architecture of the Hindu temples have a monstrosity of animals and parts of humans combined all over them, usually in very bright colors.

Hinduism and Buddhism began in India. Hindus are truly a people that worship the creature over the Creator (Rom. 1:22–25). Instead of eating a cow, they worship it. The gods of Hinduism are beyond number. Their belief in reincarnation is such that they believe they could return in the form of an animal in the next life. Thus, they do not want to kill animals. When I stayed in a hotel in Rajastan, there was a mouse in my room. The hotel attendant removed it, but only threw it outside and a short time later it was back in my room again.

When I was ministering in Delhi, I prayed for many Hindus for healing. I saw one woman fall to the ground and start to slither like a snake. I cast the demons out of her in Jesus' name and her whole family came to Christ that night.

Jesus loves Hindus and wants to set them free from

GOD VS. RELIGION

serving a multiplicity of gods. A double-minded man is unstable in all his ways (James 1:8). Polytheism is very confusing and so are the Hindus of India. I often watched them in prayer shake their heads frantically and clap excitedly trying to attract spirits to give them some spiritual experience. When people are open to spirits to this extent, they are very likely to be visited by demon spirits looking for bodies to inhabit. Jesus, the Prince of Peace, wants Hindus to know Him and be settled in their souls.

> [There] are [no] gods which are made with hands.
>
> —ACTS 19:26

Many in India carve idols with their hands, which they sell and also worship. We should lift up our hands to heaven and not waste our time making idols that cannot move or talk (Ps. 115:4–8). If you are praying to a god that cannot speak to you, then you are wasting your time. Jesus is a living God and speaks to His people (John 10:27).

Buddhism

Buddha was a kindhearted teacher who created a philosophy for others to follow. Buddha never told people to pray to or worship him. Nevertheless people have done so.

When ministering throughout Burma, Thailand and Taiwan, I encountered many Buddhists. They are sweet and very hospitable people. They do not hesitate

Dumb Doctrines and Convictions

to erect a shrine in their businesses for good luck. I learned from one former Buddhist monk in the Bible school where I taught in Burma that Buddhists greatly fear evil spirits. He told me all of the offerings, incense, and practices are to appease the spirits lest they get angry. This monk came to know Jesus and His authority, after which he left the Buddhist monastery.

He was captivated by the boldness of Christians who did not fear demon spirits. He thought to himself, *If we Buddhists are so religious and good, why are we so afraid of evil spirits?* It was then he awoke to the risen Christ who is all-powerful and mighty.

> God has not given us a spirit of fear, but of power and of love and of a sound mind.
> —2 Timothy 1:7

I once saw a Buddhist woman in an airport shuttle bus nearly jump out of her skin when a monk sat near her. Apparently, it is a huge taboo for a Buddhist woman to touch, or be touched by, a monk. Buddhist women in Southeast Asia are told that if they are good, in their next life they might get to be men.

In Christ there is no male or female (Gal. 3:28). Religion always oppresses people with fear and never affords humanity equality. Not so with Jesus who loves everybody, empowers whosoever will seek him, and considers women equally capable in the kingdom of God (John 1:12; 4:9, 27).

―― ∞ ――

Jesus is the same; yesterday, today, and forever!

God loves to rock your world.

We should never think to reduce God to our liturgical ways, denominational rigidity, or fearful conformity.

Love, life, and liberty are what God is all about. Fear and conformity are the trademarks of religion.

God's voice will quiet your soul and help you get away from religious noise.

Experts made the Titanic. Amateurs made the ark.

God enjoys anointing the unlearned and using them to change the world, while intellectuals scratch their heads and try to figure it out.

If you don't like the way the cookie crumbles, try the Bread of Life.

Religion says, "Do." Jesus says, "Done."

Religion has orphans. Christ always leads us to Father God.

God awakes you to be self-aware and empowers you to be fulfilled.

Religion strips you of your own identity. God turns identity into destiny.

Religion practices condemnation. God invites you to a divine celebration.

Chapter 11

Religion Is Static—
God Is Spontaneous!

For twenty years I attended church with my grandparents and parents who attended different denominations. The only thing I recall is struggling to stay awake during the services. As a child, the only thing I liked about my grandparents' church was that it was next to a McDonalds. Their church had an elderly lady who passed out candy to the children after church. Also, my best friend went there, and even though we did not have a lot of time to play together, it was nice to see someone I knew.

My parents' church had breakfast pastries and juice before church. Beyond those refreshments, I did not find the services to be overly refreshing or invigorating.

I was an acolyte at my parents' church during junior and senior high, but not by choice. My dad made me do it. I had to wear this long, white robe, as if it wasn't hot enough in Florida. At the beginning of the service, I had to light the candles while the organ played what sounded to me like some very still, sober funeral music. Then during the service before communion, I had to walk up to the altar and pour oil and wine for the priests. The weirdest part was this one instruction I was given, which was to pour a bit of the wine on

God vs. Religion

the priest's hands during his cleansing. It seemed to me that it would make your hands sticky. At the end of the ceremony I extinguished the candles.

By the end of the service, I was the one who felt extinguished and exhausted. Nothing said or done during the services necessarily added to me. I actually felt a bit drained by it all and was always happy to go outside when it was time to leave. I felt diminished and contained the whole time in church. It was like walking around in a straightjacket and being told what to do. I never saw any real exuberance, expression, or supernatural breakthroughs.

The big breakthrough came at the age of twenty while I was in college, when I experienced a supernatural touch from God. It was then that I began to read the Bible and feel the Holy Spirit. It was amazing! The Holy Spirit's touch and presence were electrifying. It was like hot oil rushing up and down my inner being, glory filling my soul, and fire flowing on and all around me. Indeed, there was a vast difference between God and religion. Thankfully I made this discovery. Sadly, I wasted twenty years bound and fruitless in dead religion, thinking I was pleasing God.

After my supernatural visitation, I left the dead churches I was brought up in to seek a spiritual house where God's Spirit was present and flowing in power. I came upon what some would call a charismatic church led by Pastor Benny Hinn, which was like going to a big party every service. The atmosphere was celebratory and dynamic. People who came experienced and testified of

Religion Is Static—God Is Spontaneous!

miracles in their lives. They were on fire for God. This was different from the funereal-like religious services I had been familiar with for twenty years with my family.

When my family saw me escape their church, they began to criticize and mock me. I gladly endured their criticism and remained in life-giving spirituality. I realized the people attending those churches with my family were sincere and truly desirous of God as I was when I was there. Nevertheless that did not change the condition of the churches. You cannot put a live branch on a dead tree.

> The man that wandereth out of the way of understanding shall remain in the congregation of the dead.
> —Proverbs 21:16, kjv

I had no intention of remaining in religion after having tasted divine life. Perhaps the sermons at my parents' church might have helped some, but I never sensed a spirit of faith or inspiration flowing from the pulpit. As a youth I was bored to tears there. Orlando Christian Center, Pastor Hinn's church, on the other hand, had exuberant praise and worship, people dancing and shouting for joy, fiery sermons, altar calls where people received prayer, and best of all, divine manifestations of the power of God. As a result, I developed a deep intimacy with the Holy Spirit and the Godhead.

I saw many people healed of diseases. I also saw demon-possessed people set free. Watching such occurrences live was way better than going to the movies or

God vs. Religion

going dancing at a club. I was being touched, transformed, and equipped for the ministry by watching Pastor Benny. Diving power flowed consistently in the days of Jesus. That is how it should be today.

> Jesus Christ is the same yesterday, today, and forever.
> —Hebrews 13:8

We should never think to reduce God to our liturgical ways, denominational rigidity, cultural stupidity, or fearful conformity. The Holy Spirit is the Spirit of liberty. Love, life, and liberty are what God is all about. Fear, stupidity, and conformity are the trademark of religion.

Another thing I noticed, once I escaped the prison with stained-glass windows and began attending my new church, was that people were not overly caught up in what everyone wore. It was very liberating to be loved and accepted without the uncomfortable, religious attire. Besides, nowhere in the Bible does it say Jesus ever wore a suit and tie. I am not a suit-and-tie kind of guy. I am a God kind of guy now, thanks to the marvelous discovery of the Holy Spirit and the Bible. The dead churches my family attended were without Bibles. The only person who ever seemed to have a Bible was the priest. At my new church, everyone brought their Bibles and vigorously followed along during the sermons.

There is a vast difference between religion and God. I pray that you escape the confines and tentacles of religion to discover the true and living God who loves and is crazy about you!

Religion Is Static—God Is Spontaneous!

God Likes to Laugh

It may come as a surprise, but God likes to laugh and have fun. He often does so by stretching you beyond your doubt and disbelief.

> Then Abraham fell on his face and laughed, and said in his heart, "Shall a child be born to a man who is one hundred years old? And shall Sarah, who is ninety years old, bear a child?"
> —Genesis 17:17

> Therefore Sarah laughed within herself, saying, "After I have grown old, shall I have pleasure, my lord being old also?"
> —Genesis 18:12

> And Sarah said, "God has made me laugh, and all who hear will laugh with me"
> —Genesis 21:6

God loves to rock your world, blow your mind, and do the impossible. For some reason, humans do not think outside of the box too easily. Expanding our minds and thoughts seems to be quite difficult as we are creatures of habit. God likes to take us beyond the ordinary into the extraordinary. (See Genesis 5:24; Hebrews 11:5; 2 Kings 2:11; Ezekiel 8:3; and Matthew 14:29.)

God does not get worried or bent out of shape by the wicked. Christians may fret and worry about what evil people do, but not God. Our Father in heaven knows how to turn every circumstance for the good (Rom. 8:28).

God vs. Religion

> The wicked plots against the just, and gnashes at him with his teeth. The Lord laughs at him, for He sees that his day is coming.
> —Psalm 37:12–13

> Why do the nations rage, and the people plot a vain thing? The kings of the earth set themselves, and the rulers take counsel together, against the Lord and against His Anointed, saying, "Let us break their bonds in pieces, and cast away their cords from us." He who sits in the heavens shall laugh; the Lord shall hold them in derision.
> —Psalm 2:1–4

People who mock God and His men are just comic relief to the hosts of heaven. Our God always has the last laugh and final word on everything.

> And I told them of the hand of my God which had been good upon me, and also of the king's words that he had spoken to me. So they said, "Let us rise up and build." Then they set their hands to this good work. But when Sanballat the Horonite, Tobiah the Ammonite official, and Geshem the Arab heard of it, they laughed at us and despised us, and said, "What is this thing that you are doing? Will you rebel against the king?" So I answered them, and said to them, "The God of heaven Himself will prosper us; therefore we His servants will arise and build, but you have no heritage or right or memorial in Jerusalem.
> —Nehemiah 2:18–20

God shall likewise destroy you forever; He shall

Religion Is Static—God Is Spontaneous!

> take you away, and pluck you out of your dwelling place, and uproot you from the land of the living. Selah. The righteous also shall see and fear, and shall laugh at him, saying, "Here is the man who did not make God his strength, but trusted in the abundance of his riches, and strengthened himself in his wickedness."
>
> —Psalm 52:5–7

> Indeed, they belch with their mouth; swords are in their lips; for they say, "Who hears?" But you, O Lord, shall laugh at them; you shall have all the nations in derision.
>
> —Psalm 59:7–8

God always vindicates His children. It may take awhile, but the truth always outlives a lie. If you will just hold on and wait on God, He will surely come through for you. The righteous will never be ashamed or dismayed.

> When the Lord brought back the captivity of Zion, we were like those who dream. Then was our mouth was filled with laughter, and our tongue with singing. Then they said among the nations, "The Lord has done great things for them." The Lord has done great things for us, and we are glad.
>
> —Psalm 126:1–3

The rebellious refuse to listen to God. Our patient, heavenly Father never pushes Himself on anybody. God lovingly waits until we welcome Him into our lives before He intrudes, even though He knows what is

God vs. Religion

ultimately best for us. God does, however, laugh when the wayward in heart meet up with circumstances that confirm the error of their ways.

> Because you disdained all my counsel, and would have none of my rebuke, I also will laugh at your calamity; I will mock when your terror comes.
> —Proverbs 1:25–26

When we obey God blessings surely come to us. These blessings may not occur instantaneously, but they will come when we refuse to faint.

> Blessed are you who hunger now, for you shall be filled. Blessed are you who weep now, for you shall laugh.
> —Luke 6:21

> Woe to you who are full, for you shall hunger. Woe to you who laugh now, for you shall mourn and weep.
> —Luke 6:25

God always causes His children to be victorious and rejoice in the Lord. Laughter is a key component to manifesting the fruit of the Spirit daily in our lives. Where there is laughter, there is trust in God. Where there is trust in God, there is peace and divine release.

> A time to weep, and a time to laugh; a time to mourn, and a time to dance.
> —Ecclesiastes 3:4

Religion Is Static—God Is Spontaneous!

I think more church people need to learn to rejoice in the Lord their God. If you visit City Harvest Church in Singapore, or Hillsong Church in Australia, you will encounter happy, rejoicing people. For, "Blessed is the people that know the joyful sound: they shall walk, O Lord, in the light of thy countenance" (Ps. 89:15).

The battle belongs to the Lord. It is not by might, nor by power, but by the Spirit of the Lord that we shall be victorious (Zech. 4:6). God wants us to break forth into joy and rejoice with singing (Isa. 52:9). Our God never asks us to do something He Himself would not do. When the Lord asks us to sing, He Himself leads the way.

> The Lord your God in your midst, the Mighty One, will save; He will rejoice over you with gladness, He will quiet you with His love, He will rejoice over you with singing.
> —Zephaniah 3:17

> I will declare Your name to My brethren; in the midst of the assembly I will sing praise to You.
> —Hebrews 2:12–13

> Rejoice in the Lord always: and again I say, rejoice.
> —Philippians 4:4, kjv

Love is fulfilling. Religion is never satisfied.

*God created man for relationship
and fellowship, not religion.*

*Man created religion to seek to justify and
appease his own guilty conscience.*

*Religion is man's futile attempt to
satisfy his deep, spiritual hunger apart
from God, who is the great Spirit.*

*The heart of God is continually overflowing
with loving compassion for His creation, even
when they fail Him and break His heart.*

*God forgives, because He has a heart. Religion
accuses, because it is self-righteous and throws darts.*

*Religion is full of dos and don'ts to keep you
bound and dead. God is full of wisdom and
revelation to show you the best way to get ahead.*

*Religion embalms the living with corruption
and deadness. Friendship with the Creator
in a living relationship looses the captive
and fills his heart with gladness.*

*A living relationship with the Creator
is ongoing and limitless.*

Chapter 12

Relationship Over Religion

Religion cannot give love. Only a meaningful relationship can give love. Love is fulfilling. Religion is never satisfied. God created man for relationship and fellowship, not religion. Man created religion to justify and appease his own guilty conscience. Religion is man's futile attempt to satisfy his deep spiritual hunger—which is a longing not for religion, but for relationship.

Religion is full of dos and don'ts to keep you bound and dead. God is full of wisdom and revelation to show you the best way to get ahead. Religion has dead icons and idols that want your affection. God has a heart full of blessings even when you reject Him.

The heart of God is continually overflowing with loving compassion for His creation, even when they fail Him and break His heart. A person can forgive; an entity cannot. God is a Person. Religion is a thing. God forgives, because He has a heart. Religion accuses, because it is self-righteous and throws darts.

*****

Religion: A Fatal Attraction

The God of heaven is alive and well.
He has done His all

God vs. Religion

To keep you out of hell.
He sent His Son Jesus
His one and only
To shed His sinless blood
On the cross at Calvary
To open our eyes
That we might see
To open our ears
That we might hear
To touch our hearts
Enabling us to feel
The Spirit of the living God
Raised Christ from the dead
Therefore we
Can get out of bed
For newness of life has come
Jesus paid the price for man's sin
The job is done!
Now it is up to us to realize
To remove the scales of deception
From our eyes
To walk away from religion's distraction
To not be ensnared
In its fatal attraction
For religion cannot save
Religion cannot heal
Religion cannot touch
It is not even real.
Religion is the creation of man
Whose years are limited
Why then with religion

Relationship Over Religion

Should you be riveted?
Get up you sleeper
Awake my friend
For religion wants to keep you
Until the end
But if you continue
Apart from God
Religion will take you
To the depths of hell
Where Satan dwells
Then your end will be
Clearly seen and revealed
For religion is worthless
Poisonous to the core
Deadly in all its dealings
While you innocently explore
Take one taste
And now another
In religion
There are no sisters and brothers
Religion is for spiritual orphans
Who don't desire a family of faith
Religion is for intellectuals
Who don't want to live by faith
There is however one problem
Religion does not tell you your fate
That it keeps you from heaven's gate
From heaven's blessings
Which can be experienced here on Earth
In Christ through the new birth.
Religion however is a lie without worth.

God vs. Religion

Abraham was a friend of God (James 2:23). Friendship with God, the Creator of heaven and Earth, is reason to celebrate! Religion has no celebration, no new songs to sing, and no shouts to give. Religion embalms the living with corruption and deadness. Friendship with the Creator in a living relationship looses the captive and fills his heart with gladness—this is every Christian's job. Jesus raised Lazarus from the dead, but He told the disciples to loose Lazarus (John 11:43–44). We, too, must arise and loose those bound in religion so that they can be free.

Before Jesus raised Lazarus from the dead, His disciples took away the stone from the place where he was laid (John 11:41). Today we must take away the stones of religion that have kept people enslaved, bound, and dead within. As we do, our God will arise and cause them to be born again in newness of life in Christ.

A living relationship with the Creator is ongoing and limitless. Religion, man's creation, has a beginning and ending. There is no beginning nor ending to the Creator, who dwells with and inhabits the hearts of humanity. God is awesome and endless in power, wisdom, and love. All His goodness from above He makes available to us because of His love.

You do not need to be mesmerized or left empty by religion. All your heart's desires can be satisfied through a relationship with the living God. Let go of religion and be filled to overflowing by cultivating a relationship with Him.

Let go of the mere mental reasoning of religion and enter the realm of supernatural feeling and knowing

Relationship Over Religion

by the Spirit of God. Go from cerebral to spiritual. Stop chasing religion in the wilderness, and let your heavenly Father lead you into your personal promised land to obtain your inheritance. You can have more in life if you stop settling for less. Get some courage and leave the coffin of religion and the corpse it has made you. Religious ritual bores, binds, and breaks you down. A relationship of love with the Creator lifts, liberates, and launches you into your dreams. The choice is yours. Jesus said, "Follow Me!" (Matt. 4:19). The Master is leading the procession out of religion for you and me. The exodus is on. Leave religion and, in God, become all you dream to be.

The Lord our God is high and lifted up, far above and beyond religion. Jesus died for you, so you can die to religion. Look unto Jesus and live! Jesus redeemed us from self, sin, and sadness. Give your life to Christ to experience freedom and joyful gladness!

Pray out loud with me now:

> *Wonderful Jesus, thank You for dying for me! Thank You for opening my eyes and heart to clearly see. Please forgive me for my sins, religious ignorance, and arrogance. Cleanse me with Your blood, and remove all religious madness. Send now Your Holy Spirit to resurrect me within and impart divine gladness. Come now, Holy Spirit, to lead and guide me. Introduce me to my heavenly Father and Jesus so I can live in victory! Amen.*

As a fish feeds on a lure thinking it is food, so do many feed on foul, dead religion expecting to be nourished.

Religion wants you to work until you bleed. God wants you to look unto Him and believe. Religiosity is full of formality because it is void of spirituality and spontaneity. Religion is continually critical. The Holy Spirit is patient and helpful.

Religion is based on fear, ignorance, and insecurity. It teaches you to discipline yourself to be a better person. God in heaven touches you by His Spirit, and recreates you as a new person.

Religion is full of accusation and condemnation. God is full of loving acceptance and reconciliation. God created the Sabbath for man as a day of rest, but religion only wants to question, debate, and test.

God created humanity for relationship and fellowship, not for religion. Religion has orphans, but God always has sons and daughters. Religion strips you of your own identity. God turns identity into destiny. Religion practices condemnation. God invites you to a divine celebration.

Notes

Introduction

1. Web site: jmm.aaa.net.au/articles/3815.htm, accessed September 18, 2006.

1—Misrepresentations of the Master

1. Web site: www.churchofsatan.com/pages/ninestatements.html, accessed October 3, 2006.

2—Fig Leaves of Self-Sufficiency

1. Dr. Mark I. Chironna, *You Can Let Go Now: It's OK to Be Who You Are* (Nashville, TN: Thomas Nelson, 2004).

10—Dumb Doctrines and Convictions

1. *Strong's Concordance* (Grand Rapids, MI: Zondervan Co., 2001).

Contact the Author

Paul and Karla Davis can be contacted for professional speaking, consulting, coaching (professional and relational), conflict resolution, restoring order (professional organizing) and much more.

>   Paul & Karla Davis
>   Dream-Maker Inc.
>   PO Box 684
>   Goldenrod, FL 32733 USA
>   407-284-1705; 407-967-7553
>
>   RevivingNations@yahoo.com
>   www.DreamMakerMinistries.com
>   www.CreativeCommunications.TV
>   www.PaulnKarla.com